# BREAKING
## IN THE NEWS

*Build Buzz for Your Brand*

# ALISON MALONI

# To my girls

When I wanted to quit, I thought of you. When I was too tired to write anymore, I thought of you. When I finished this book, I thought of you. You, my babies, are the reason for everything I do. Thank you for supporting me throughout this process. Thank you for giving me some quiet time to write. Thank you for believing in me. And thank you for being you. You are my sunshine, my only sunshine. I love you.

# Contents

# Foreword

I knew that beautiful, brilliant nine-year-old girl with the bright future Alison describes in her first chapter. Since she was a little girl, I have always admired Alison's drive and determination. While other girls were playing with Barbies or hanging out with friends, Alison spent much of her childhood visiting a newsroom, joining me for speeches in the community, and envisioning her seat at a future anchor desk, as she sat on my lap visiting the TV Station. Alison kept her personal promise to herself to climb that ladder of success. She made it to the top of her field in both broadcasting and PR and now she's sharing her advice to help others.

This book is a must-read for anyone wanting to learn PR and how to work with the media. Read on to learn Alison's PR tips and techniques as she shares her secrets for any business, service, or organization to get noticed in a competitive media landscape. Alison knows what she's writing about—she's lived it both in front of the camera and behind the scenes. If you want to improve an image and get media attention, this book provides a step-by-step process to a successful PR campaign. Her candid, clever advice will make a difference for anyone who takes the time to read her book. I couldn't be more proud of watching Alison—a confident, goal-oriented girl who grew up to be a powerful PR professional and most importantly, a mother of three beautiful, bold girls who are watching her career and all the triumphs and hardships that come with a drive to succeed. Learn from Alison's amazing stories—and watch your own business thrive.

*Brenda Garton-Sjoberg*

Former News Anchor and Professor of Communication at WNE

# Introduction

The Teen Bop magazines were pushed aside to make the white desk look clean and professional. The pink, green, and blue carbon-copy news scripts—along with my carefully crafted news stories—were the only thing that sat in front of me. I carefully taped a border on my wall that was supposed to look like a video camera so I could have a focus point. Next to me was a tall lamp I borrowed from our living room to shine a light on my face. I wore a red shirt and borrowed a black blazer with big shoulder pads from my mom's closet. Under my mom's red shirt was a bra stuffed with socks. Making my hazel eyes sparkle was a light shade of green eye shadow and a little too much eyeliner. After borrowing a bright red lipstick from my mom, I was camera ready.

I had spent the afternoon reading newspapers, writing scripts, and memorizing every word. My prep work was done, and it was almost showtime. A few seconds before the clock struck five, I played a pre-recorded tape on my small pink boombox that said, "Five, four, three, two, one, and we're live." It was time to broadcast.

I would then say, "Good evening, everyone. I'm Alison Maloni, and welcome to Springfield's news station. Here is the top story of the night."

That was me at the age of nine every single day. While other kids were playing Nintendo, I was writing news scripts and pretending to broadcast the news from my bedroom. If I got in trouble, my parents would take away my nightly broadcast, and I couldn't watch the news. Yes, I was that kid.

Fast forward thirty years later, and I'm anchoring the news from a real studio with better lighting, a slightly different wardrobe, an unstuffed bra, and much better makeup. It's funny how things become a reality when you imagine them in your mind and are determined to make them happen. But getting there was not easy. Nothing is, right?

I had recently turned forty. My public relations business was finally starting to take off, and my three daughters were thriving. However, I was about to make the biggest decision of my life. I was getting a divorce and starting back out on my own. I was terrified of so many things. *Will my girls be okay? How will I support myself on just my income? What if I lose clients? Am I making the right decision?*

In life, I believe you have to face your fears head-on. Whether it's your personal or professional life, it's so important to take the chance, take the risk, take the bull by the horns, and do it.

So that's just what I did. There were certainly tough times, but as I look back, it was the little victories that I was so proud of. I was paying my bills on my own, taking out the trash, shoveling the snow, and getting it done. Were there breakdowns? Heck yes. Do I still have breakdowns? Heck yes. I am the first to admit that I struggle with so many things in life, and anyone who paints their life as perfect is lying.

Fast forward a few years, I went through another tragic event in my life. I was on the verge of losing clients and was in debt. I fell into a depression. I would hide in my shower to cry. I couldn't eat, and I honestly don't know how I made it out of bed.

Through the support of my best friends and family, I got up from the couch and took it one day at a time. Sometimes, it would be one hour at a time. Doing my hair and putting on makeup would be a victory in itself. But it didn't just happen overnight; it took weeks, months, and years to heal. I am not sure I will ever be completely healed, but I know that everything happens for a reason.

As I moved forward, I knew that I needed to put myself and my company out there. I had to take the advice that I give my clients, which was to pitch yourself and your company to the media. It was now or never. For once, I put myself and my company first. I began doing video blogs every day. I was writing a blog a week and pitching myself to multiple media outlets. From PR and marketing media to women in business and motherhood stories, I pitched myself.

After a lot of hard work, I began to see the results with media coverage and increased engagement on social media, along with new clients.

Now that I had established myself, I was given the opportunity that I had wanted since I was nine years old: to be on the network news. At the age of forty-three, I was a contributor to a national news network and anchoring shows in New York. I remember one day I was walking down the hallway of the studio, and I felt an overwhelming feeling that I couldn't explain. All I could think was, *Oh my God, I am here. I have wanted this for over thirty years.* I didn't ever think it would happen, and after everything I had gone through, I was here. For once in my life, I was truly proud of myself.

Things were great, and then, COVID-19 hit. I still had my public relations agency, but we began to lose clients. I was doing the news from home, but I knew that it was not a full-time gig. The kids were home from school, and like everyone else, we had to pivot.

Outside spending of companies was cut, and we had to figure out how to stay open, pay the bills, and still help people get media exposure.

We launched a digital course on how to build your brand and get media exposure, and that's where this book was born.

There are so many startups, entrepreneurs, and new businesses out there that can't afford an agency, and I know how important media exposure is. I know how it can help take businesses to the next level. I know how it can change lives.

I have put all of my tips and knowledge from being a journalist, publicist, and business owner in this short, simple book—something you can read quickly and apply immediately to your business.

While there is a ton of information here, it's only good if you do the work. It is all up to you, and if you put in the work, I guarantee you will see an increase in your media exposure.

Back to that broken single mom, she began doing what a lot of people weren't doing. Now, it's time for you to do what everyone else is NOT doing.

*"If you don't tell your story, someone else will." – Unknown*

LET'S DO THIS.

# Chapter 1
# What is Public Relations?

*"If a young man tells his date how handsome, smart, and successful he is, that's advertising. If the young man tells his date she's intelligent, looks lovely, and is a great conversationalist, he's saying the right things to the right person, and that's marketing. If someone else tells the young woman how handsome, smart, and successful her date is, that's PR."*
   *– S. H. Simmons*

When I first started my public relations firm, I met with a marketing agency to team up on a project. We sat down to discuss how we could work together, and the CEO explained to me that the agency didn't personally handle public relations because they didn't quite understand it. He had assumed that public relations was just writing press releases and holding events. The CEO said that he had always put public relations in the same category as marketing and advertising. This was not the only time I heard this from marketing firms and CEOs.

A lot of people don't truly know what public relations is, but I will tell you that *every* company and thought leader needs it. First, let's talk about what PR is not. It's not advertising, it's not marketing, and it's not sales.

Now, here's what PR is: Public relations is about the many ways you communicate with the people in your audience. It's the stories you tell, the relationships you build, and the press you earn to help people positively connect with your brand.

The great thing about public relations is that it is free media exposure. With advertising, you have to spend a lot of money, hope that your target audience sees it, and pray that it works. If you get media coverage, you do not pay for it. Someone else is talking about your brand and story, and you can promote the media coverage, which builds your reputation.

# PRO TIP

Seth Denson, Co-Founder & Chief Strategist at GDP Advisors:

"Back in 2018, a story broke within the business sector that would have significant ramifications both to the financial markets and to the specific industry (in this case, healthcare) that would be impacted. A local reporter, who I had never met, got my name as someone who may be able to comment on the story. They reached out, and I responded. My response was so well received that, later that day, my comments made it to the national scene as I was contacted by Fox News to do a segment on Fox Radio. The next morning, my phone was lighting up with friends, colleagues, and clients who said they had 'heard me on the news.' That experience was quite literally the game changer for both me and my firm, and once I had gotten a taste of being a commentator in the media, I quickly found myself wanting more.

PR has helped solidify my brand. I subscribe to the belief that only I can control my brand, but PR helps me amplify it. Time is the great equalizer for all, and engaging with a professional PR firm has allowed me to utilize my time most effectively and efficiently, which is honing, researching, and developing my craft. Knowledge leads to confidence, confidence leads to enthusiasm, and enthusiasm sells. If you want to be on TV, you're constantly having to sell yourself, and enthusiasm is a key component. Without a great PR firm, I would have had little ability to invest the time and effort to develop that knowledge base, which ultimately led to my ability to constantly sell myself while on-air."

The more a brand or thought leader is in the media, the more they are respectively perceived as the product to buy or an expert in the business. Perception becomes reality.

# The ROI

Let's break this down to a dollar amount. We recently got a client on a national morning show.

As publicists, we knew that his story had what journalists call "legs" (meaning it had major potential). He got a two-and-a-half-minute segment on the couch with all three of the morning anchors (this was pre-COVID). During that time, his website crashed from so many people going on the site. Within a few hours, he had thousands of emails from other business owners in support of what he was doing. He booked ten new client appointments throughout the country within two hours of his interview. Since then, he has been asked to be on the news, other national media outlets have interviewed him, and his client base has increased significantly.

If you were to buy a television commercial during the number one–rated morning news show, you are talking about thousands of dollars for a thirty-second advertisement.

But if you appear on the news for a 2.5-minute segment, then it is on the national news website, along with social media channels and your outreach, which equates to nearly a hundred thousand dollars' worth of advertising. In the public's eye, you are the expert, your company has a great story, and your product is a must-have.

Wreaths Across America, an organization that ensures a wreath is on every gravestone in Arlington National Cemetery for the holiday season, was struggling to get donations that would allow them to continue this tradition. The story was sent to Fox & Friends, and shortly after, the network invited Bre Kingsbury of Wreaths Across America to come on and share their story and mission. Bre explained they were short of donations, which meant that not every grave at Arlington would receive a wreath. After the story aired, Americans came out in droves to help, including a bank that donated $100,000 to make this possible. Fox & Friends then invited Bre and the donor to come on air to do a follow-up story. Because this story initially aired,

Wreaths Across America was able to raise the funds it needed to ensure that every one of our hero's graves received a wreath. Besides, more American's knew about the organization and spread the word about what they do. This is a prime example of how public relations can impact an organization—all because of one story.

While Wreaths Across America saw huge success with the segment being on TV, this does not always bring people knocking down your door to do business. We hear all the time from people that want to be in the news so they can increase sales. This does happen, but it is typically not an overnight process. It also depends on if you are positioning yourself as an expert or your product/service is being highlighted in the media. Public relations is part of the puzzle: it works with your marketing, sales, and advertising.

# PRO TIP

Seth Denson, Co-Founder & Chief Strategist at GDP Advisors:

*"I can count on one hand the number of prospective clients that have called me wanting to do business with my firm because they saw me on the news. That said, there have been several times I've walked into a prospect meeting and been recognized as 'that guy on the news,' which always seems to give me the upper hand. Validation is a great asset, and third-party validation is the best kind—when a national media outlet tells the world you are an expert, it's hard to argue that. Content on the world wide web is huge as well. If you don't think your clients and prospects are Googling you, then you're grossly mistaken... they probably are, and when you Google me, you can find a lot of content—positive content. When they Google my competition, they might find a website or a LinkedIn page. Content is key, validation is key, and when those are put together, it's powerful."*

*It is great to be the guy or gal on the news, but when you are planning out your public-relations strategy, you must be focusing on all aspects of your company and personal brand. Content is king, and being in the media will help establish you as an expert, but you must be patient and consistent."*

# Chapter Roundup

- PR is a way to communicate with your audience
- PR is storytelling and not advertising
- PR can significantly change your business and brand
- Are you convinced yet that you need to do PR for your brand or yourself?
- Would you believe it if I told you that it is not that difficult?
- Let's dive in and teach you how to be a pro in no time

# Chapter 2
# Get Your Social Media in Check

*"We're living at a time when attention is the new currency. Those who insert themselves into as many channels as possible look set to capture the most value."*

    *– Pete Cashmore, Founder of Mashable.com*

Walk before you run. If you are like me, once you get an idea, you want to go full steam ahead. I get so excited about something that I tend to forget the all-important planning. Before you do anything, let's make sure that your messaging is on point.

I had a consult call with a potential client who just launched their company. They were super excited to tell the world about their product and would have shouted from the rooftops if they could. Their website looked great, but their social media needed work. They had a few posts on Instagram and about a hundred followers. When I looked at their social media, I didn't see their story. What are their core values? What's their brand? They also didn't post very often or respond to the comments on their page. I wanted to learn more about them, and if I was a journalist looking at their social media, I would be asking the same questions.

After I looked at their social media, I gave them a descriptive explanation of what they needed to do to build their brand and utilize social media. I encouraged them to strategize, build their brand, and then tell their story on Instagram, Facebook, and Twitter. Just like public relations, social media is all about storytelling and connecting with your audience.

Why is branding so important? Because whether it is a company or personal brand, customers, clients, future employees, and the media connect with brands. They want to know exactly what they are getting from a company or a thought leader.

# PRO TIP

Susie Ippolito, Owner of SI Brands:

*"Social media is an opportunity for every brand to have a 5th Avenue storefront. Brands tend to underestimate the valuable connections they can make on social media. The mistake I most often see—especially in new brands—is that they don't take the time in research and development to properly test their ideas. Before brands go to social media, they need to learn how to articulate their value and the problem they solve in clear and concrete terms. This takes a minimum of three months of research into who your brand is and how it creates value for the larger world.*

*There are many important questions brands need to ask themselves:*

- *What problem does our product solve?*
- *What other available solutions are there?*
- *How do these solutions make customers happy?*
- *Where are customers unhappy with available solutions?*
- *How does our product exceed customer expectations?*
- *How do we solve this problem differently and better than any other solution?"*

People are going to a company's social media before they go to their website. A company could have the best product, but if they don't have a consistent and clear message and story on social media, that could heavily impact the brand.

Think about what you do when you look up a company. If they have a lousy social media account or poor reviews, what do you do? You probably keep searching for a different company, product, or restaurant to go to.

Think of your social media accounts as your house or apartment. If you are having company over for a special event, you will most likely spend the day cleaning and organizing. When your guests arrive, you may use your favorite wine glasses and have fresh flowers on display and candles burning. You want them to get a great impression of you and your home. The same amount of thought and work should go into your social media pages. It's a home that is always open for visitors. Your social media pages should be authentic, relatable, and inspirational.

## PRO TIP

Sabrina Reilly, Reporter at Fox, CBS, & ABC affiliates:

*"I am a journalist who hates going into interviews blindly. Time is valuable and limited when it comes to turning a story. That's why, before every interview, I always take my time to research the company or expert I'll be speaking with. That said, time is valuable, and as a reporter, I don't have enough of it! When a company has an excellent website and social media presence, it allows me to better weed through the unnecessary and find the story that matters and the company that can speak to it.*

*Additionally—as a multimedia reporter who often ventures to stories alone—I want to make sure the company or expert I am calling is someone I can trust. Let's say I am tasked with finding a local plow company that is seeing a boost in business due to an increase in snowfall this winter. The first thing I do is turn to Google. Based on my search results, I start cold calling companies that I find to be reliable, trustworthy, and well established based on the information I find online. Without proper promotion in the form of a website or social media, it can be next to impossible to catch my or my fellow journalists' attention."*

## Step 1: Update Your Website

While a lot of eyeballs are on your social media channels, it's still important to have a clean, crisp, and up-to-date website. You will want to hyperlink your site in your pitch or press releases, and that may be the first place that journalists go.

- Ensure that your website is updated
- Make it consistent with the rest of your branding
- Check for broken links
- Update your media page to include any recent media clips and segments
- If you have videos about your brand, add them to your site. Journalists love seeing how you do on camera

## Step 2: Google Yourself

Have you ever Googled yourself? It may surprise you to find out where your company or your name appears on the internet: any article that has been written about you, videos that you have done or appeared in, photos, social media…you name it.

It's always a good idea to see what's out there regarding you or your brand. You can set up a Google Alert with your name and brand so anytime there is something with your name(s) online, you will know about it. It's a great way to track your media coverage too.

## Step 3: Audit Your Social Media

Your social media is just as important as your website when you are pitching to the media. Journalists and potential customers go to your social media to scope you out, which is why you want to make the best first impression.

Pull up all of your social media accounts and check to ensure your logo, color, and font are all consistent. Then, go through your posts and ensure that they represent your brand and identity. Whether you are a company or an expert in your industry, you may want to tweak them or even delete some older posts. I always recommend that you stay away from political or controversial posts unless your goal is to take a serious stance on an issue and get media exposure over that.

## Step 4: The Social Media Lowdown

Now that your audit is done, are you on all of the right social media platforms? Some platforms work better for certain brands. Let's dive in.

# Instagram

This is one of the fastest-growing social media platforms. In 2020, there were 1 billion active users on Instagram. This is a must for all brands: health, beauty, fitness, food, drinks, gifts, fashion, accessories, travel... you name it. If you are an expert or influencer, you want your profile to be a professional headshot from the shoulders up and to create an informative bio. It's important to check your Instagram insights, which give you all of your stats.

## How Often to Post

### Feed

You should post at least once a day. Mix up your posts with photos, graphics, Instagram TV, and Reels. Reels have been performing extremely well on Instagram, and you can share them on Pinterest to attract even more attention. Reels are only 15-second videos that you put to audio and text. It is really important to engage with your audience on your posts. Create posts that ask them questions and respond to all of their comments.

### Stories

If you are going to focus on anything on Instagram, your stories should be the top priority. More people look at stories than feeds. According to Instagram itself, more than 500 million people use stories daily, and one-third of the most-viewed stories come from brands.

You should post on your story multiple times a day. Your stories are an in-the-moment video or picture. This is when you can highlight your product, show behind the scenes, inspire, and be authentic.

# PRO TIP

Gina DiStefano, CEO of MomBombs:

*"Mom Bomb is a luxury bath and body product company that exists to fund a 501C3 charity. As such, all of the profits that Mom Bomb makes are sent to our sister 501C3 and are used to provide grants for mothers in need. Having mothers buy into our mission of women helping women was crucial for our growth.*

*Finding the right method of communicating with our audience took some trial and error. At first, we thought irreverent, sarcastic anecdotes about motherhood would resonate, but it didn't. We then decided to better understand our audience via connecting with our target demographic and asking them what they liked. We created a Facebook group and began just connecting on a personal level with the participants. Over time, we were able to see trends, pick up on topics important to our audience, speak directly to the people who would most likely buy our products, and see the differentiating factor for why we exist. We researched other brands and how they spoke to their audience and came up with a way of speaking to this group that resonated. We found that equating motherhood to "heart work" was a compelling tagline that embodied both why we get up and serve women every day and what our target audience feels about motherhood. With that, we created a strategy around communicating topics to our audience that they could not only identify with but that strengthened our brand messaging at the same time. The response has been overwhelming.*

*We were willing to share our own stories of loss, stress, and overcoming immense traumas that drive us to continue this mission, and through that authenticity, we attracted consumers that also identified with us. Sharing our experiences was the single best way to express that we, just like them, are also just trying to keep our heads above water. We too are hot messes. This relatability translates into brand loyalty every time."*

### Best Time to Post

According to Sprout Social, the best time to post is Wednesday at 11 a.m. and Friday from 10 a.m.–11 a.m.

Looking at Instagram as a whole, the most consistent engagement can be found Monday through Friday, 9 a.m.–4 p.m., but engagement is also high on weekends.

# LinkedIn

This is not as important for brands, but for individuals, business owners, thought leaders, experts, media personalities, and speakers, you should have a presence on this business professional platform. A professional headshot and a detailed bio are key.

## How Often to Post

On your LinkedIn feed, you should post once a day Monday through Friday. LinkedIn is primarily a business platform, and they have fewer active users during the weekend. Videos also perform very well on this platform. If you post informative quick video tips and mix them up with photos and great advice, you can grow your audience pretty quickly. LinkedIn is a great place to build your professional/personal brand.

### Stories

LinkedIn has followed suit with Instagram and Facebook to create stories. They have not caught on as well as Instagram, but I expect people to be using them more often. Posting a few times a day is a good goal for this platform.

# Facebook

Facebook tends to generate an older demographic. In the U.S., the average age of a Facebook user is 40 years old. While other social media platforms are growing in popularity, Facebook is still important to be on.

## How Often to Post

I follow the same as Instagram by posting at least once a day on your feed. Mix up your videos and photos to show variety.

## Stories

You should do the same amount as you do on Instagram. You have a setting on Instagram that will automatically post your story to your Facebook story.

## Best Time to Post

There have been studies about when the best time to post. According to Sprout Social, the best times are 11 a.m. and 1–2 p.m.

# Twitter

This is *the* platform for journalists. Nearly every journalist and media outlet are on Twitter, and while you may not think it's going to increase your audience, you want to have a Twitter profile because it will help you with media exposure. This is such a great place to find journalists, connect with them, and eventually share the stories they do on you.

## Feed

If you are trying to be relevant and attract media attention, then you should be posting on Twitter multiple times a day. Share stories from media outlets and journalists whom you respect.

## Best Time to Post

Monday through Friday between 8 a.m. and 4 p.m. tend to work the best.

# YouTube

If you are looking to be an influencer or thought leader you should think about setting up a YouTube channel. YouTube continues to grow and there is a space for almost every industry. Your channel needs to look professional. I recommend investing in a good camera, lighting, background, and microphone.

# TikTok

This is not for everyone, and it depends on your product and your audience. TikTok is geared toward a younger audience (teens–20-year-olds). According to Statista, as of June 2020, users in their teens accounted for 32.5 percent of TikTok's active user accounts in the United States. According to App Ape, users aged 20 to 29 years were the second-largest user group, accounting for 29.5 percent of the video-sharing app's user base on the Android platform, but it's gaining users in an older age range. I recommend that you pay attention to this. If it makes sense for you and your company to jump on the TikTok bandwagon, do it and have fun with it.

# Pinterest

This is a great platform to be on if you are a retailer, chef, blogger, fashion designer, or beauty brand. Like TikTok and YouTube, there are no optional times to post.

# Chapter Roundup

- Do a social media audit
- Ensure your branding is clean and consistent
- Google yourself and company
- Be on the social media platforms that are appropriate for your brand
- Consistently post on your social media platforms

# Chapter 3
# The Strategy

*"Strategy is a fancy word for coming up with a long-term plan and putting it into action." Ellie Pidot*

I believe in creating strategies for nearly everything, but I also know that they have to be fluid, especially in PR. 2020 is a prime example. When COVID hit, every business was affected and had to pivot. Just like nearly every business in America, we were affected by COVID. We lost our biggest client. I had to let go of one of my account managers, and I was just praying the rest of our clients would hang on and stick with us.

Before you start telling your story and reaching out to the media, you want to make sure that you are pitching to the right media and know where your audience is. For example, if you are an organic snack company, you will want to focus on the health and wellness media industry, think about podcasts in your space, and reach out to social media influencers who can promote your product.

Before you start your strategy, ask yourself these questions:

- Where is your target audience?
- What type of media do they consume?
- What media outlets do you want to be on?
- Who will be your spokesperson? Is he/she energetic and comfortable on camera?

You can and should have goals to be in big media outlets, but I want you to think about starting small and having realistic goals in the beginning. PR takes time.

When you create your strategy and pitch to the media, think like a journalist. A journalist is always thinking, "Why would my readers or viewers care about this story? Why is it important to them? What is different about this story? How will this help the audience?"

The first part of your strategy is figuring out if you want local press, industry press, national press, or all of it—and you definitely can have all of it—but remember, start small.

# 12-month Strategy

- Write down what is important in your industry.
- Think about what you can talk to the media about.
- Take each month and go through what you could potentially pitch to the media: holiday gift ideas, holidays, industry trends, new product launches. Keep in mind that magazines are three–four months ahead. For example, if you want your product to be featured in their holiday guide you should pitch them in August.
- Create a content list. This is a list of topics that you can write about as a guest contributor; try to pitch one topic a month to the media outlet that you choose. We will talk more about this later in the book.

# Pro Tip

Jen Berson, Owner of Jeneration PR

> *"Having a PR strategy is important for a small business so they can establish goals and work strategically toward them.*
>
> *A PR plan should include your goals, which are essentially your primary outcomes or your 'dreams' for your business. It should also detail the strategy for how you will achieve your goals. A press plan should include objectives that are measurable steps you will take as part of your overall strategy to achieve your goals. Finally, consider the specific tactics, which are the tools you will use and the actions you will take to meet your objectives.*
>
> *It should be somewhat detailed but flexible so the strategy can easily be adjusted if a tactic isn't working, or your goals change over time."*

# Lead Times

When you are working on this strategy, keep in mind the lead times in the media that you are pitching to. National print magazines have long leads, which means writers and editors are working on stories three to four months in advance. If you want your product to be featured in a summertime roundup, then you should pitch in January or February. Digital media outlets have shorter lead times, usually about a month in advance. This is why it's extremely important to have a strategy in place.

# Chapter Roundup

- Know who your audience is
- Create a strategy
- Plan out your pitches
- Create a list of articles you can write

# Chapter 4
# Local Press

## Local TV News

*"Local news taught me to take each moment as one of extreme importance—don't waste people's time. Give them solid information in a compelling fashion so they will remember it and use it in their lives."*
*- Harris Faulkner*

I am sure that, in your PR strategy, there are large national media outlets on your list, and those are great goals to have, but as I have said before, it is important to start small and build from there. Depending on where you live, your local media may not be as small as you think.

As a former local news reporter and now contributor and anchor for a national news outlet, I have had the chance to sit in on editorial and producer meetings. Unless you are in the newsroom, it's hard to understand how the crazy world of news works. It is not like any other industry, and it's very important to know how the industry works before you pitch to them. If you have that first-hand knowledge, the local reporters and assignment editors will recognize it, and that's big bonus points for you.

## The Ins and Outs of Local News

Local news stations have general assignment reporters (which means they report on everything from breaking news to feel-good stories). In larger markets, there are beat reporters that focus on political, investigative, and health stories. When you are researching the news station or newspaper, it's important to look for this so you know who to send your pitch to.

In local television news, the reporters typically do two stories a day. They only have a few hours to interview, write, and edit the story, and many times, they do all of this in the field and report live on the story for the newscast.

Local newspapers have similar reporters assigned to stories as the television stations. Their deadline is usually the day of as well, but for feature stories, the deadlines are a little longer. All year round, you pitch yourself to speak about a newsworthy topic, and if the news station is interested, they will want to speak to you that day—usually within a few hours of receiving your pitch.

Here's how it works: let's say, at 8 a.m., you let the media know you wish to talk about a certain topic. They would have a meeting at 9 a.m., and the reporter would call you at 9:30 wanting to interview you by 11 a.m. that day. The story would then air in their evening newscast. It's fast, and that's why it's essential that if you pitch yourself or your company to the media, *you must* be ready to speak on camera that day... within hours.

# PRO TIP

Jen Berson, Jeneration PR:

*"When it comes to appearing on national TV, it is essential that you gain experience in local and regional TV segments first. National outlets will want to see that you are telegenic and can carry a segment and that you won't 'freeze' on TV when the lights go on! You can build a reel of your appearances to show how you are on camera and include that with a pitch to national media—or have it at the ready if they ask. You could even use Facebook or Instagram 'Lives' as the start of your reel to show a local TV network how you perform on camera. I always tell clients to dream big and aim high for their media goals but know that press is cumulative and you will build momentum when you start small, see what resonates with smaller media outlets, then position yourself and your brand to national media with your best foot forward!"*

If you didn't pitch yourself but the media happens to call you to talk about a specific topic in your area of expertise, say yes. Reschedule your appointments. Make time to meet with the media. If you say no, they will move on to someone else... maybe even to your competition.

## PRO TIP

Seth Denson, Co-Founder & Chief Strategist at GDP Advisors

*"Soon after my 'one-hit wonder' in 2018, I recognized that there was significant value in presenting myself as a subject-matter expert. I engaged with a PR firm that specialized in our local market here in Dallas as well as national radio. That provided me the ability to 'cut my teeth' and learn how to manage my mind and my mouth at the same time while being interviewed. There's no question that the six months I spent doing local news and national radio helped me lay the foundation for what I get to do today.*

*By the fall of 2018, I got my national TV break. A story specific to my expertise was making national headlines, and I was contacted by Fox News to join Fox & Friends to discuss. The segment went so well the producer for one of the weekend shows called me immediately after to request I join them to discuss the same issue. The next year, I did nearly 100 national television segments across multiple media outlets."*

A former colleague of mine who is still in the news business will call me every once in a while, looking to see if I have any clients who can weigh in on different topics. She will always say that they called numerous people, but they were apprehensive about doing the interview or wouldn't change their schedule. She would finish her story by saying, "Don't they understand that this is free advertising for them?"

I think, many times, people get nervous that they are not fully prepared for the interview. You don't need to know everything about everything. As long as you understand your industry and enough about the story that they want to talk to you about, you will do great!

If you can do the interview, that could open doors to other opportunities. When journalists find an expert that is knowledgeable and has a good presence on camera, they can become the go-to person on the topic.

For example, travel stories are something that can be covered all year round. In one market I worked, we made cold calls to travel agents, and one made herself available within our tight deadline. Due to her availability and her ease on camera, we called her on other occasions for other travel stories.

# PRO-TIP

Shawana Perry, Media Manager at WPVI:

*"Just to give you an idea of what a typical day in a newsroom is like, the moment a journalist gets approval, there is a countdown clock that constantly reminds them there is a limited amount of time before their deadline. Here is a possible breakdown of their day: In a perfect world, a reporter can get their assignment between 9:30 a.m and 10:30 a.m. If their story is on television at 4:00 p.m., they are setting a goal to send their script in for approval by 3:00 at the latest, which means they need to talk to you by 1:30 p.m. When journalists are making those calls on same-day stories, they are looking for you to be available within two hours. When adding breaking news into the mix, they are hoping you will be ready the instant you answer the phone. You must remember you are not the only person they need to get this story on the air. For people outside of the news business, it will feel like you are trying to run a marathon in five minutes."*

If you are nervous, the important thing to remember is that a good journalist will make you feel comfortable; just have an open mind and relax.

Reporters understand people are not going to be available every time they call, but if you do not want to do the interview or cannot, let them know as soon as possible. This allows them to make their next phone call to meet the deadline.

If you have agreed to do the interview and it is on a tight deadline, it can take a total of fifteen minutes; this includes setting up the equipment. In most instances, it may take you longer to get to the interview than to do the interview.

In the world of virtual interviews, it may take even less time. To help make this process go smoothly, ask which app they use, check your internet connection, make sure you have good lighting, and find a quiet area. If you need to use your phone, you should not hold it in your hand during the interview. Find something that can prop it up, so it is not shaking during the interview. If that happens, it could lead to your interview not getting used.

I have worked in different television markets, and there are key things that happen everywhere that many journalists find frustrating. Two examples come to mind:

First, if you reach out to a television media outlet, please remember you will be on camera. I have heard too many times people say, "Oh, I thought I could just tell you my information without you recording me." In our digital age, all media platforms are using video to help tell stories, so you or your voice will be on the record if you agree to the interview.

Second, if you send a news release about an event you want to be covered, do not be cryptic about your information because that could result in you not getting coverage. If you want the information to be withheld until your announcement, consider using an embargo. This will prevent the information from being published until the designated time.

# How to Find Local Television Contacts

Building your media list is fairly easy. You can simply go to your local television's website, search under the "Contact Us" button, and there is usually a list of email addresses. You will want to look for the assignment editor's contact information. There is usually a general email address, which is fine, but I would go a step further. If the email address is not specific to the assignment desk, just call the newsroom and ask who the assignment editors are, what shifts they work, and what their email addresses are. This way, you have their direct contact information. You should also add all of the reporter's contact information to your media list because you can send your pitch to them, but I always recommend starting with the assignment desk.

# How to Find Local Newspaper Contacts

To find contacts for your local newspaper, you can also go to their website and look under the "Contact Us" section. You will see editors and writers for specific beats. Be sure to only email the editor or reporter that is specific to your industry and what they cover.

## PRO TIP

Shawana Perry, Media Manager at WPVI:

*"When it comes to pitching stories to a newsroom, do not make it feel like a commercial; instead, think about the relevance to the news of the day. We can get a hundred emails in an hour, and we need to grasp what you can offer quickly.*

*If you have a distribution list for your news release, send it to the newsroom assignment desk email account because there is always someone looking at that inbox. As a favor to every newsroom in America, double-check your distribution list to make sure you are not sending the email more than once to the same address. There are times when journalists will give the assignment desk email address to contacts, but organizations, companies, and legislators do not realize they have multiple names for the same address. It starts to feel like spam, and it may be overlooked."*

When I was at WPRI in Providence, Rhode Island, we saw a story about interest rates going up nationally. We reached out to a local realtor to talk about how this will impact the housing market locally. They knew we were on a tight deadline and made themselves available. They even met us at a house that was for sale so we could have that for the background of the interview. It was a fantastic interview, and we were done in just fifteen minutes.

Months later, there was another housing story that we wanted to do, so guess who we called to talk about it. That realtor moved her schedule to talk to us before, so she soon became a regular expert on the station.

If you say yes and do a good job, they will look to call you the next time they need an expert in your industry to speak to. The reporter will even share your contact information with other reporters in the newsroom if they are looking to do a story related to your industry.

# What the Local News Looks For

## Current Topics and Experts

The local news is always looking for experts to talk about what is happening in the area. If you can speak about current topics or trends in your industry, this is your opportunity to inform them and explain how it affects their audience. For example, January is typically a time where people focus on New Year's resolutions. If your company makes a non-alcoholic beverage, this would be a great time to reach out to the media to talk about ways people can have a "Dry January" while enjoying a mocktail. It's really important to pay attention to what is going on in the news, both locally and nationally, so you can pitch yourself and your story to the media.

When I was working in local news, there was a national story about a proposed tax hike for small businesses. We reached out to a few area business owners to see if they would talk about how this would impact them. We must have called a dozen and only one called us back. We immediately interviewed the owner and learned more about her business. A few months later we were looking for small business owners to talk to again. Guess who we called? The business owner who spoke to us about the taxes. She soon became a regular expert on the news.

Everything takes time. It took about a year of sending out pitches (once a month or more) to the local media before an anchor on a local news station asked, "Do you want to come on the noon show once a week?" I said, "Yes!" and was on the show weekly for three years!

If you can get an interview on a news show, I think it's important to be flexible, reliable, and as easy to work with as possible. I always emailed them a list of bullet points and even suggested an "intro" for the topic along with any applicable photos or videos, so they never had to do any work for my segment. They always let me choose my topic— I think because they trusted me for being so thorough.

# PRO TIP

Ashley Brodeur, MS, CFSS
Owner, Active Lifestyle Fitness, LLC:

*"I worked with Alison to come up with ideas to send to different media outlets. She sent them out, and we waited to see who replied! We usually went for topics related to whatever was happening at the time. For example, if it was starting to get hot outside, we would send something out about exercising safely in the heat, or if we were doing a fundraiser in February for women's heart health, we let the media know about that too.*

*It's very important to pay attention to trends and stories in your industry because if you're not the first to step forward and say, 'Hey! I know about this! Come talk to me!' then someone else will!"*

*"I do remember, one time, I picked a topic about squash, and as I was watching the teasers for the show, I noticed they had pre-recorded a segment with a local farm also about squash! I contacted the anchor and asked if he wanted me to change my topic, and he said that would probably be a good idea. I came into the studio about an hour later for my live segment with a completely new topic. The production crew and the anchor were shocked I could put together something so quickly, but I believe putting in the effort and showing them that you care about their show is what helps build the relationship that keeps them calling you back!*

*"Sometimes, you hit it off with a journalist, and sometimes, it flops. Like anything else, you can't take it personally if they don't come back to you, but when you do hit it off, cultivate the relationship as much as possible! Interact with them on social media. Like, comment, and share their posts. Always stay top of mind and show them that you care about them as people. For example, one of the anchors with whom I became close acquaintances was pregnant while I was doing weekly health and fitness segments, so I did a whole six-week block of segments just about pregnancy. If I was doing healthy cooking segments, I would try to find out what the anchors liked to eat so I could incorporate those items.*

*I also had a fitness instructor that worked for me who became a journalist for the other local station. She calls me often because she knows me and my business, and she also gives my name to other journalists for interviews. In my opinion, it's important to stay on good terms with everyone you work with because you never know where they will end up!"*

## Localize National Stories

The local media likes to localize national stories if they affect their audience. For example, how many times did you see local doctors on your news being interviewed about COVID-19? Even before it started to spread to my state, Massachusetts, the local news was talking to infectious disease doctors about how to stop the spread and symptoms.

When I worked for local television in Massachusetts, there was a national story about a chain restaurant that had an outbreak of E. coli. While it wasn't spreading in our area, we wanted to talk to a local doctor about what E. coli was, how it's transmitted, and what the symptoms were. We called a doctor's office where we have done interviews before, and they immediately provided us with a doctor to talk to. We initially called that office because they had always come through for us and gave us doctors to talk to at the last minute. They knew how local television worked, and it was a great way for the practice to get their name out there.

# How Interviews Work

Most of the time, the interview is not live, and the reporter will come to you. The key is to have what's called a "b-roll" for the reporter. "B-roll" is a video that the photographer or the reporter will take after your interview. It will be used to cover some of your interviews when the reporter is telling the story.

Don't be surprised if the reporter shows up alone and is both the reporter and the photographer. Many local news stations have created positions for reporters called multimedia journalists, which means they do everything! This is a very tough job, and I give them a lot of credit. If a multimedia reporter comes to interview, anything that you can do to make their job easier will go a long way.

When journalists are putting together the story, they are always thinking of what video is going to be in the segment. Keep this in mind when you are getting ready for your interview. It's always great to have a good background to interview in front of and think about the type of video they can get at your business. For example, if you are a chef, they will want to get a video of your restaurant and show you cooking and interacting with the staff, etc. Mainly, they will want a video to go along with whatever it is you are talking about. It can also be photos that you have taken too.

# You're Going Live

You may get asked to do a live interview. They typically occur during the morning or afternoon shows. For local news, if you are in the studio, it is a lighter story. You may cook for one of their segments, or if you are a personal trainer, you could do a sample workout with one of the anchors. Don't let the word 'live' scare you. Believe it or not, it's easier to do live interviews than taped! I think we have in our minds that there is no stop recording button, so we only have one shot.

When you are prepping for your interview, which I will cover in a later chapter, just practice. Stand in front of a mirror and pretend that you are doing the live interview. I practice all of the time. I do it in the car, in front of the mirror—anywhere I can.

# Don't Forget Social Media

When you are filming the interview, don't forget to have someone take photos and video of you being interviewed for social media. This is extremely important as more people will see it on social media and tune in to see your segment. Always be thinking about social media content and your reputation.

The local news is a great place to begin building your reputation and presence; plus, it gives you the experience and confidence of being interviewed on camera.

# Chapter Roundup

- Local news is the best place to begin your PR efforts
- When pitching to television stations reach out to assignment editors
- Local news likes to localize national stories. Always pitch yourself as an expert in that subject matter
- If the news wants to interview you, make yourself available

# Chapter 5
# Industry News

*"Nobody counts the number of ads you run; they just remember the impression you make."*
  *– Bill Bernbach, advertising pioneer and founder of DDB*

When I started my company and needed to get clients, I was pitching myself like crazy to every media outlet I could. I knew that the more I was in the media, the more I would be perceived as a thought leader. The result is that people want to do business with experts, and if they are featured in the media, it does put you at a higher level than your competitors.

I knew that I needed to show my skills as a publicist and journalist. The best way to do that was to appear in PR, marketing, branding, social media, industry-focused digital media, and blogs.

So, let's get you in these outlets too!

Industry news can be blogs, trade publications, and digital media. There are media outlets in pretty much every industry. From finance and food to knitting and collectibles, you will probably find a media source that covers your industry. Who else knows your industry better than you? Remember, you're an expert. You can talk about what is happening in your industry to those who consume that media. If you see something in your industry that you can talk about, pitch it right away to the media.

A lot of people think that it doesn't make sense to be featured in industry media because their customers or clients are not reading it— just their competitors—but you do want to be in these outlets. You gain credibility by being quoted in industry media outlets and that's exactly what you want. It's all about what you do with the press coverage once you receive it. Perception becomes reality.

Besides, there are so many chances for you to be quoted in industry-focused media. Most likely, there is a podcast or digital media source that covers your expertise. Take some time to research who they are and pitch your story ideas to them. It's a great way to get recognized and build your media credibility.

Before we get into how to appear in these outlets, let's talk about ways you can be featured.

# Guest Writer

This is a huge one. Digital media outlets are constantly turning over new stories. Many digital outlets are looking for guest contributors. All you have to do is pitch a topic, and if they approve, they will send you the guidelines. The main thing to think about when writing your article is to not be "salesey" or to overly promote your product or service. Your article is all about providing value and education to the readers. This is a great way to build the portfolio of your press.

You then become a thought leader, and your brand becomes legitimized. This positions you as an expert in your field, and you then become the go-to person to talk to about your subject. Plus, any press mentions can be shared on social media, which will increase your following and bring more people to your website.

If you are not a strong writer, you can hire a copywriter for a reasonable rate on Upwork, and it will be well worth it. You will likely have an author bio at the top or bottom of the article along with a link to your website and social media accounts.

# A Story on You or Your Company

If you have an interesting story that you believe the audience will benefit from, this is a great opportunity to pitch a journalist to write about you.

## Expertise

Journalists are always looking for experts for their stories, and they typically feature a few different ones in their articles. While this is not a full article that you write or a story dedicated to you and your company, I believe this is a great way to get on journalists' speed dial

(Do we even have a speed dial anymore? I'm dating myself here!), but you are a huge asset to journalists as they need experts to explain the elements of the story, and once you are quoted, you have a relationship with the journalist, and it opens the door for other opportunities.

Now, let's get you in these media outlets!

## Where Do You Want to Be?

Identify a list of industry media that you would like to write for or be featured in. Bigger isn't always better, especially when you start out. Just as television news, you should start small and build up your credibility.

Finding these media outlets and blogs is pretty simple. You are probably already following some of them. The best way to build a list is to do a Google search outlining your industry plus the word "blogs," such as "food blogs" and "political blogs. Many media outlets such as Huffington Post, Thrive Global, Entrepreneur, Business Insider, AdWeek, Fast Company, Forbes, Venture Beat, Hubspot, Success, Money Saving Mom, and Mashable take contributors.

## Build Your Media List

Create a Google Doc or spreadsheet and start adding the media outlet name, the contacts, and the social media handle. You can find their contacts by going to their website and looking under "Contact Us." Some blogs and media outlets have listed contacts, and that would be the first place to go. Some blogs also have "Write for Us" or "Guest Post" sections. That is where you would submit your article.

There are cases where media outlets do not have the journalist's contact information, but there's always a way!

1. Good Old Google – Sometimes, it's as simple as a Google search. Journalists may have a personal website that includes their contact info.
2. Find them on Twitter – Nearly every journalist is on Twitter, and they sometimes have their contact info in their bio.
3. Search LinkedIn – You may invite them here to connect. If they do, you can start a conversation.

4. Use MuckRack – This is a platform where there's a collection of journalists. It's possible to obtain journalists' contact info straight from there.

## Writing Your Article

It's important to scroll through the blogs and media outlets to see what's been written so you are not duplicating it. You can always elaborate on an article that has been written but try to think of something unique.

Here are a few things to consider when coming up with an article idea:

● Write a "how-to" article

● Write about an industry trend

● Explain a newsworthy topic

Every media outlet is different as far as what they would like for an article. Some just want you to send them an outline of an article while others want the entire piece written. Before you submit it, have a colleague review it for grammatical errors. Also, send that specific article to only one media outlet at a time. They want unique and unpublished articles for their sites. A good rule of thumb is that if you don't hear from them in a week, you can send that article to another source.

## The Pitch

I will get into the details of a pitch and subject line in a few chapters, but the key is to create a personalized pitch that is going to get the attention of the journalist. They get hundreds of pitches a day, so you want to make it stand out. Don't do a mass pitch and "bcc" hundreds of journalists. They can recognize that and want your article to be specific to their media outlet. The best days to send pitches are Tuesdays, Wednesdays, and Thursdays, and the best time to send pitches is between 10 a.m. and 4 p.m.

## Follow Up

I can't tell you how many times I receive pitches with no follow ups. Here's why follow ups are so important: I may see a good pitch, but

I'm on deadline for the news and will forget about it; it gets lost in my email abyss. However, if you connect with me the next day or two days later, you are back on my mind. By reminding them of yourself, by bringing up the email, you're giving yourself another shot.

# Chapter Roundup

- Industry media outlets will help establish you as an expert and thought leader
- You can write an article, pitch yourself as an expert, and share your story with a journalist to potentially be featured
- Create a list of contacts using Google, Twitter, LinkedIn, and Muck Rack
- Write a compelling pitch that will stand out
- Don't forget to follow up
- Submit your article to one media outlet or blog at a time

# Chapter 6
# Digital Media/Print
# Publications

*"It's PR that needs to be creative. It's PR that needs to be new and different. It's PR that needs to be original. The best way to establish a brand is to create a new category, and creating a new category requires creative thinking of the highest order." – Al & Laura Ries*

I remember my client was featured in Entrepreneur Magazine, and he took the article and framed it on his wall. He was ecstatic, and who wouldn't be? What an achievement! And here's the thing: he is not a multi-million-dollar company. He's not a famous CEO. He's a business owner with a good story and had a really good pitch. He started in local news, moved on to industry media, and moved into bigger digital media outlets like Entrepreneur Magazine.

And you can too.

Let's talk about digital. Some digital media outlets are strictly online while others are a combination of print and digital. From your local business publication to Forbes and Yahoo Finance, they are all online. Their lead time can be anywhere from the same day you pitch the story idea to a week or two out. It depends on what the journalist is working on. What do I mean by lead time? It's the amount of time that the magazine needs in the production process to go from a writer's pitched idea to the published version of the magazine.

Many of them have editorial calendars, which is where they plan out the year to cover specific topics. They are usually located on the media's website. This will help as you plan to pitch them or pitch an article that you can write about. You will find the editorial calendars on the media's website. These are extremely helpful as you plan out your pitches.

One of the biggest things to pay attention to is lead times. I mentioned this in a previous chapter but understanding the difference between short and long lead times will help you pitch your story.

## PRO TIP

Jen Berson, Jeneration PR:

*"When you pitch the media, you need to think about the lead times for long and short lead publications. Long leads are monthly print magazines that are typically considered and writing content four months out, and short leads are digital publications as well as daily newspapers and weekly publications. They typically work about three–four weeks out. There are, of course, some exceptions, like for breaking news, which will be quickly considered and included in the media almost immediately. Other exceptions are long-lead holiday gift guides, which are typically in the works six months in advance! Yes, six months! These issues typically take a lot of time to compile as they are considering hundreds or thousands of products for their gift recommendations, so if you want a chance to have your brand and products featured in a December gift guide, you need to send your pitch in July!"*

One of my clients has a skin care line, and we wanted to get the sunscreen pitch to the beauty editors in time for their summer issues. We sent the pitch in January, and we heard back that it would be in their May issue, which was amazing news, and that's why it's so important to have this inside knowledge as to how the news works.

Just like industry media and blogs, the major magazines love to have guest writers. As the need for content continues to grow, these outlets are working to generate fresh content online 24/7, and your articles can help them. While you typically don't get paid, it's a great opportunity because you are controlling the message. Plus, you are featured in the news, and you can share it on all of your social media platforms. It's a win for everyone!

A newer trend in journalism is freelance writers. As media outlets are working to put out fresh content 24/7, they need more writers to contribute, and it ends up costing them less as they pay freelancers per story. The great thing about freelancers is that they write for multiple media outlets, and once you establish a relationship with them, you could be featured in many news outlets.

# PRO TIP

Kelsey Ogletree, Freelance Journalist:

*"A freelance writer is someone who runs their own business that just happens to be writing. They make a living by pitching ideas to editors who then commission them to write articles for their publications. Many successful freelancers work with 10+ publications at the same time. The benefits to pitching freelance writers (and building a relationship with them) over editors are great. Here are a few:*

- *They tend to be more accessible and responsive as they're not tasked with other duties of publishing a website or print publication.*

- *They are their own boss, so they get to decide to whom and what ideas they pitch.*

- *Because they write for multiple publications, they provide the potential opportunity for more than one angle of coverage.*

- *Ideas are their livelihood, so continually sending a freelance writer solid ideas is a great way to build a relationship and thereby increase your chances of being included in more stories.*

*Many people overthink a pitch to freelance writers or never pitch at all. Just like in hockey, though, you'll miss 100 percent of the shots you don't take. Keep pitching—set a goal for yourself to do it every day—until you send one that lands."*

*"Freelance writers vary in what they prefer to have included in a pitch, but there are some general rules:*

*Use your subject-line real estate wisely. Be specific and consider writing your idea headline style and in the format of the publication you'd love to be in.*

*Keep it short and to the point. What is the actual story idea? Just because something exists doesn't mean it's a story. Present the unique angle in five sentences or less and include a hyperlink to more information.*

*Include a timely hook. Why that writer? Why cover this now? Your pitch should answer these questions.*

*Specify why it's a fit for that writer's publication(s). Why should their audience care about this idea? Be sure your pitch answers this concisely."*

Digital media outlets and magazines love doing top five or ten roundups. For example, you can expect to see a story in February from a magazine about the top Valentine's gifts to give your lover or, in January, the top ten fitness gadgets we can't live without. There is also something to be said about feeling, seeing, or trying a product. Set aside samples to send to key journalists.

# PRO TIP

Kelsey Ogletree, Freelance Journalist:

*"Some products are simply better experienced. If you have a food item, a perfume, a beauty product, or something else that can be touched, smelled, tasted, etc., it's a great idea to send a product sample via mail to journalists. Being able to experience a product can leave a much greater impression than a simple email about that product.*

*If you're considering a mailer, be sure to vet who you're sending it to first. Have they covered other products in this space previously? Do they write about your industry? Have they ever posted on social media about products they've tried? If the answers to those questions are yes, they could be a good person to connect with. "*

*"Reach out via email to ask if they're familiar with your item, and if they're open to receiving a sample, ask them to share their mailing address. Be sure to send along tracking information so they know when to expect the package. Give them a little time to interact with the product (say, at least one week) and then follow up to ask for their thoughts. Including a card in the mailer that lists social handles for you or your company is a great idea if you're interested in social media coverage.*

*If you don't have a specific idea to pitch a freelance writer, that's okay! Simply reaching out to introduce yourself and your company, brand, product, etc., is a great way to begin a relationship that can develop into a pitch down the road. Say hello, let them know you've read some of their work, and mention what you liked about a piece or two. Taking a genuine interest in that writer as a person; showing your personal side as well goes a long way. You may also wish to follow a freelance writer on social media for a while before pitching them to get a feel for what they are all about and what they cover.*

*When pitching and working with freelance writers, be sure to manage your expectations. Great stories take time. Sending one product sample does not guarantee coverage. The higher the caliber of the outlet and writer you're targeting, the greater lead time and collaboration you should expect. It's rare that a freelance writer will receive an email pitch and immediately turn around to pitch a story to their editor. It can take months or even years to bring a feature story to fruition. Look at working with freelance writers as an opportunity to build relationships that will bring benefits to both sides and maybe even develop into a friendship for years to come."*

# Op-Eds

Another great way to get noticed in the media is by writing an op-ed, an opinion article.

If you really want to take a stance on an issue, an op-ed is the way to go. There are many benefits to writing an op-ed: If you get published, it shows that you are an authority on a particular topic, and it makes you more marketable to the media. This positions you as a thought leader in your industry, which is exactly what all this is intended to do. Most op-eds have a word limit, which means you have to be succinct and efficient. Every media outlet has their own submission guidelines. You can find all of that information on their website.

One important point to remember is that, with op-eds and any information you share with the media, it is there forever, so always have someone else read your response or article before you submit it. You need a second or even third set of eyes before it goes live into the world.

## PRO TIP:

Mark Vargas, Political Strategist:

*"Opinion pieces are highly effective because the writer is controlling the narrative. Every word is yours, and in the media, that's very important. Like an artist, you've got a blank canvas, and the freedom to paint or write whatever you want.*

*Opinion pieces, if published in credible publications, can give you instant credibility on any topic that you are writing about. You are the expert, and readers will look to your piece for information, insight, and analysis. Opinion pieces also play an important role toward branding because it expands your visibility and name ID. It gives you a platform and a voice that many do not have."*

*"Writing op-eds has been life-changing for me personally. It's given me a voice and a platform that I never had before, and through writing, it's connected me with incredible people. A piece that I wrote about modernizing government technology led me to connecting with billionaire entrepreneur Mark Cuban; a piece that I wrote about the need to reform a broken and racist criminal justice system led me to corresponding with Jared Kushner, president Trump's son-in-law, who was leading the White House effort on criminal justice reform at the time; and a piece that I published on the Rod Blagojevich case set in motion a two-year campaign that ultimately led to President Trump commuting his prison sentence.*

*Talk to anybody who writes often, and they will tell you the same thing: writing is hard, and writer's block is real! But if you add passion, expertise, and good research, the final product will be something that you'll be proud of, and others will enjoy it too.*

*Op-ed writing is very different from regular writing: It has its own writing style, and you've got to keep it brief—500–700 words and no more. Submit your op-ed to various publications that you personally read and follow and don't give up if you don't hear back from them. Keep trying, look for email addresses of the opinion editors, and email them directly. Don't waste your time sending your articles to generic email addresses—find real people with real addresses and make sure that your pieces are relevant. Tie your article back to anything that's dominating the news cycle."*

# Chapter Roundup

- Digital and print media have short and long lead times. Short lead times can be as early as a few days and weeks whereas long lead time can be four–six months. That is why planning is so important to get featured in these media outlets

- Freelancers should become your best friends. More news outlets are using freelancers to write their stories. The great thing is these journalists write for multiple media sources. Once you establish a relationship with them, you could be quoted in many outlets

- Op-eds are a great way to get your voice heard. They tend to be more difficult to get picked up in, but if you have a good article the editors think will generate a lot of readers, you are in

# Pictures in the News

OUR CHRISTMAS PARTY AT NEWSMAX.

THE ORIGINAL CREW OF AMERICAN AGENDA.

ALWAYS COME CAMERA READY OR BRING YOUR MAKEUP TO THE
TELEVISION STUDIO. THIS WAS WHEN I WAS FILMING WITH ERIC
BOWLING FOR THE BLAZE IN WASHINGTON, DC.

CARLEY SHIMKUS, FOX NEWS

ASHLEY BRODEUR, ACTIVE LIFESTYLE FITNESS FILMING A COOKING
SEGMENT ON WESTERN MASS NEWS.
LOCAL NEWS LOVES COOKING SEGMENTS.

GUYS NEED MAKEUP TOO. SETH DENSON, GDP ADVISORS GETTING
READY FOR HIS SEGMENT ON NEWSMAX IN NEW YORK.

CHRISSY MONACO, MONACO FORD SHARING THE IMPORTANCE OF
THEIR SAFETY CAMPAIGN.

MY SECOND JOB IN TV AS A PRODUCER
AT WESTERN MASS NEWS, 1999.

If you don't have someone with you during your interview, ask a producer or staff member to take a quick photo. In the photo, Alison Maloni and Eric Bolling.

LIVE TV IS FLUID AND WHEN YOU ARE A GUEST YOU HAVE TO BE
PREPARED TO THINK ON YOUR FEET.
BREAKING NEWS CAN HAPPEN AT ANY TIME.

I FINALLY GOT TO MEET JOHN BACHMAN IN PERSON WHEN HE CAME TO THE NY STUDIO. JOHN GAVE ME A CHANCE ON HIS SHOW AND I OWE HIM THE WORLD.

I APPEARED ON DR. OZ THROUGH AN OPPORTUNITY I SAW
ON HELP A REPORTER OUT (HARO).

SPEND A DAY FILMING VARIOUS VIDEOS FOR CONTENT THAT YOU
CAN USE ON SOCIAL MEDIA.

BEHIND THE SCENES. ANCHORS DON'T HAVE A LOT OF TIME TO
PREPARE FOR THE SHOW. YOU TAKE EVERY MOMENT YOU CAN GET,
EVEN IN THE MAKEUP CHAIR. MAUREEN WALSH IS THE MOST
AMAZING MAKEUP ARTIST. AS YOU CAN SEE, IT TAKES A LOT!

ROB FINNERTY, RICH GRENELL, EMMA RECKENBERG, SHAUN
KRAISMAN, ALISON MALONI

MY DAUGHTER, ADDISON ON SET AT NEWSMAX

# Chapter 7
# Podcasts

*"A podcast gives you an arena to show your expertise and passion for your niche. Your enthusiasm and speaking prowess also add an authoritative air to the topic, something that the written word cannot express, and coming out with regular podcasts that have sound information and good ideas helps establish you and your brand as market leaders."*
*- Staff, WebProNews*

Do you listen to podcasts? Check out these stats. According to Brandtastic,

- Over 55% of the US population have listened to a podcast
- In 2020, over 155 million people listen to a podcast every week
- Around 24% of the US population (68 million) listen to multiple podcasts weekly
- Podcast listeners consume an average of seven different shows per week
- There are over 700,000 active podcasts and 29 million podcast episodes

I do not need to tell you that podcasts are a huge platform to be on. As you can see, more and more people are now listening to podcasts, and it can help get you noticed by tons of listeners.

Podcasts are a great place to get your feet wet for network news interviews. The more podcasts you do, the more comfortable and confident you will be in front of a microphone.

I personally love podcasts; your personality can really shine, and they are very conversational. Just like industry media, there are endless podcasts. From true crime to comedy, news, and opinion, there is something for everyone.

According to Brandtastic, in 2021, the top five categories for podcasts are society & culture, business, comedy, health, and news & politics. Podcasts offer deep dives into the minds of industry thought leaders through interviews. In less than an hour per day, listeners can become industry experts on their favorite topics.

One of my clients went on his first podcast a few years ago, and he absolutely loved it. He described it as a cocktail party without the cocktails. He was able to show his personality and provide value to the listeners. After the podcast aired, he received a few calls from people interested in working with him because they heard him on that podcast!

Similar to industry and digital media, you have to find the podcasts that you want to be on, find the contacts, and pitch the host or producer.

Podcasts tend to book out weeks in advance, so if you pitch them to be on as a guest, they will most likely book you in a few weeks. The great thing about podcasts is that you get a decent amount of time to tell your story and weigh in on the topic.

There are tens of thousands of podcasts out there, and it can be difficult to find the best ones for you, but we use a software called Podcast Clout. Created by former journalist and publicist Christina Nicholson, it builds targeted podcast pitch lists and weeds through all the ones that aren't broadcasting consistently or have a very small audience. My agency loves it, and anyone can sign up for it. https://podcastclout.com/

Being a guest on a podcast instantly builds your authority and credibility with listeners for these two reasons.

Then, throughout the interview process, listeners don't just get to hear more about you and your expertise, but they get to hear the way you speak—therefore, get to know your personality. There really isn't another form of media where you can share that much to connect with potential customers or clients.

# PRO TIP

Christina Nicholson, Owner of Media Maven
Founder of Podcast Clout
Content Creator at Christina All Day

*"People who listen to podcasts are very invested in what they're hearing. They have a different mindset than when they scroll through online articles or have a TV on in the background. Choosing a podcast to listen to for thirty minutes or so is a very intentional thing, so already, you know the listener is engaged and paying close attention.*

*Then, factor in that the listener most likely feels like he or she knows, likes, and trusts the podcast host. By default, the listener is going to extend that known, like, trust factor to you because you are a guest chosen by the podcast host. It's almost like a referral: 'Hey, I'm a fan of this person, so you should be too.'*

*Then, throughout the interview process, listeners don't just get to hear more about you and your expertise, but they get to hear the way you speak—therefore, get to know your personality. There really isn't another form of media where you can share that much to connect with potential customers or clients.*

*It's exciting to see how much and how fast podcasts are growing. I think we saw this and started recognizing it more when celebrities started getting into the podcasting game. Many of them have their own podcasts to control a narrative and build their brands.*

*Podcasts are also very easy to listen to. Every phone comes with a podcast app; you can stream them online, you can also listen from a smart device, and they're free to listen to.*

*After being a guest on a variety of podcasts for a couple of years, I started my own podcast called **Become a Media Maven**. For the podcaster, it's very inexpensive and can take as much time as you are willing to commit to it. Some people have daily podcasts while others release one episode a week.*

*Some podcast episodes are short, and some are longer. As a podcaster, you call the shots, so your show can be whatever you want it to be.*

*Because podcast listeners are so much more engaged on the medium, if they enjoy the episode, they may seek you out afterwards. Personally, I've seen my email list grow by leaps and bounds after sharing a resource on a podcast. Then, they enter an email nurture sequence where they get to learn even more about me and what I do. In addition, people will connect with me on social media to tell me they liked the episode or will come find my podcast and subscribe to it where they listen to podcasts.*

*With more than 100 different podcast categories to choose from when you listen or come on as a guest, the possibilities for success are endless."*

When you get on a podcast, make sure you promote the episode and the host on all of your social media platforms, including your email, and encourage your employees to share it out too.

# Chapter Roundup

- More than 55% of people listen to podcasts
- Podcasts are a great way to get your message out and establish expertise
- There are thousands of podcasts out there to be on; focus on the ones that make sense for you. Just like all media, you will have to create a pitch and send it to the host or producer Save time by using Podcast Clout to find the top podcasts and contacts
- Once you are on a podcast, promote it on all your social media channels

# Chapter 8
# The #1 Way to Get
# Press Coverage

*"It is always a risk to speak to the press: they are likely to report what you say."- Hubert H. Humphrey*

This is a publicist's little secret. We like to hold on to this gem because it helps us get numerous press hits for clients. I can say that my agency has gotten hundreds of press hits using this free source.

If you take away anything from this book, this is it: It's called HARO, Help a Reporter Out. This is an online service that you should subscribe to, and it's free. Here's how it works: journalists from across the world post stories that they are working on and who they need to interview. When you sign up, you can pick categories that are in your wheelhouse. They have the technology, business, health, and fitness, and general category. You will receive an email three times a day with different stories, and all you do is read the query. If you can answer a reporter's questions, then you have a chance to be quoted in an article, be on a podcast, and potentially be on national TV. We have secured hundreds of press placements using HARO, and the great thing is you can then establish a relationship with the reporter or editor and potentially get additional press coverage. Here are a few things to keep in mind:

1. If you answer the query, it is not a guarantee that you get placement. It is very important to check your email once you receive it and respond to the query right away.
2. Ignore the deadline because they will start to immediately go through the responses, and if you give them what they want and are at the top of their inbox, it gives you a leg up.

3.  Sometimes, it doesn't say the media outlet. Don't let that sway you away from not responding. Sometimes, bigger media outlets do this so they won't get inundated with responses.

4.  Pay close attention to what they are looking for. If they are asking for a few sentences, give them a few sentences, not a novel.

5.  Many times, they will use your quote and won't let you know that the article is live. Be sure to track the article a few days past the deadline. If they give you the name of the outlet and reporter, just Google that along with the topic. You may be surprised to see they quoted you.

6.  If the story you respond to is for a TV segment, podcast, or phone interview and they want to interview you, be sure to make it easy to schedule your time. They are on deadline, and they won't have much wiggle room.

7.  If you receive press coverage, don't forget to share the story, podcast, or article on social media and tag the reporter and media outlet. There is no greater compliment for a journalist than when you share their stories.

When I was trying to build my brand and get media exposure, I found HARO and started pitching myself for business, parenting, marketing, and public relations stories. I was willing to talk about pretty much anything and put myself out there. I began to get traction from HARO, and that is what really launched my personal brand as an expert, along with my own articles and videos.

I strongly encourage you sign up for HARO. It will help boost your media exposure, and I promise it is worth your time!

# PRO TIP

Mike Tourville, author of **Voices from the Fallen: True Stories of Addiction, Grief, Recovery and Courage**

*"It's been interesting to see the variety of topics, some very curious and thought-provoking. So many times, I'd see an inquiry and say, 'Hmm, I never thought about that!' At first, I was looking for topics directly related to my areas of interest but then recognized indirect opportunities as a way of gaining exposure from an audience I may never have otherwise reached.*

*Example: For my book, **Voices from the Fallen**, I was looking for reporters interested in stories about heroin or alcohol addiction. I wasn't sure how the message in my book could contribute or add value for a reporter, but I kept an open mind. Then, I saw an inquiry looking for examples of press releases (for no specific topic), and having just sent out a press release (which had been updated with suggestions from your presentation), I thought, 'Let's see if this meets the standard and qualities they are looking for.' I received an answer within hours saying it would be used in the article as an example of a well-written press release! I would have never reached those readers if I stuck to my particular topic. I answered another inquiry asking about experiences with 'second acts' or taking chances on starting a second or third career completely different from the first. Again, unrelated to the topic of addiction, but it was an opportunity to mention the writing as a third act and possibly promote the book.*

*The lesson learned here is don't narrowly limit yourself to only your area of expertise. Think creatively about how you might add value in unexpected ways.*

*Aside from that, I suggested HARO to my daughter-in-law who is in the mortgage business to sign up after seeing several inquiries looking for mortgage experts for articles about buying a home or refinancing. She's had a good experience so far and knows that whenever she gets an opportunity, it will give her added credibility and a competitive edge. She's keeping it a secret from her local competition!*

*Within a month of signing up, I received a positive reply and was included in an article. I also received other polite acknowledgements saying, 'Thanks, we'll keep your info and may use it in a subsequent article.' I check every single email (three times a day) because I know the one I miss is a potential missed opportunity.*

*This has been a huge asset for me. First, you can't beat the price!*

*Second, each inquiry responded to might lead to national exposure from a source you'd never think to approach. There are hundreds, thousands of reporters you would never know about or ever have access to otherwise.*

*Also, it might be smart to keep the contact info for reporters that write about your topic of interest and check in with them once in a while. Be proactive and make your own inquiries. You don't have to wait for them to reach out and hope you get noticed among the hundreds of others competing for their attention. Become a 'go to' person for future projects.*

*And on that note, off the HARO topic, if someone is looking for local PR opportunities, I've found local reporters to be surprisingly receptive to writing about topics that affect their community, same for TV shows or local news.*

*It may be promoting a local author, a new business, a service... or even providing 'expert' advice relating to current events.*

*Two examples: if mortgage-rate drops are announced on the news, a mortgage-loan officer might get in touch with a paper (or TV station) to offer advice or write a brief article, or when temperatures drop to sub-zero, a plumber might offer advice about ways to prevent pipes from freezing.*

*Get to know the reporters, and you can be the one they go to when the time is right. It builds credibility and sets you up as the local expert."*

I really don't need to say much more about HARO other than if you do nothing else, use this service to help you get press. You will be amazed at what you see.

Are you convinced yet to sign up for HARO? I'm telling you: it is the best kept secret, and if you use it right, you will start to see press exposure.

# Chapter Roundup

- Subscribe to HARO (Help a Reporter Out)
- Respond to queries that are beyond your industry, such as parenting, fitness, cooking, or anything that you can talk about
- Respond right away to the queries
- Keep track of the queries that you have answered

# Chapter 9
# How to Get in the National Media

*"Publicity is critical. A good PR story is infinitely more effective than a front-page ad." – Richard Branson*

Since I was nine years old, my dream was to be a network anchor. When I graduated college, I thought I would work at a few small television stations and, by 25, I would make it to the network. I quickly realized I had a lot of work to do to get to that level.

We've talked about how to get on local TV, write for industry media, and get featured on podcasts. The next step is to start getting noticed on national TV.

Of course, there is always the exception if you have that "wow" story or a relevant news topic that has affected your brand; then, you could get national press. However, it's rare to get that level of attention, so let's focus on the following steps.

Remember, public relations is not just about getting on TV or appearing in a digital publication. You can gain credibility in multiple ways, including writing your content, creating videos, and being present and engaged on social media. All the following will help you get to the national network.

## Company PR

You want to have your company or product featured in as many media outlets as possible, and small is okay. You will also want to have a strong presence on social media. Editors and bookers will look at your social media and the type of press your brand has received.

# Personal PR

It's important to have some interviews under your belt. The more experience you get, the more you will become confident and comfortable on camera, on live interviews, and in writing. One thing that the national media bookers, producers, and editors look at is how experienced you are. Where have you been featured, what have you written, and what does your social media profile look like? Are you active in conversations online? Remember, use HARO; this will help you significantly.

# Write. Write. Write.

The media is a 24/7 business, and their goal is to put out as much content as possible. Many media outlets have made cuts, and that has opened the doors for contributing writers. This is a great opportunity for you! You have the chance to share your expertise in an article in which you can control the content and narrative for a major media outlet. Simply go on the media outlet's website and see what the requirements are to be a contributing writer. When you are pitching to the national media and they see that you have written for your industry media, that gives you credibility.

Another way to get your message out to the public is to write your blog and share it on all of your social media platforms. Just like contributing, this is a great way to show your expertise and provide people with valuable information.

# Videos

In addition to writing, you can produce videos that focus on your expertise. Keep them short, around a minute to two minutes. It's really important to let your personality come out in these. People need to be able to relate to you, and it must come across as if you are providing valuable information and not selling anything. When producing your videos, have a good DSLR camera or your phone. The key is to have good quality video, great lighting (a ring light is a top choice), and a nice background. You do not need to invest thousands of dollars to do these. As long as they look clean and professional, you are golden.

When I first began doing video blogs, I invested a lot of money to work with a professional video service to produce the videos. They came out beautifully, and I was thrilled to share them on social media, thinking I would get a ton of response from them. It turns out I got very little response. I was baffled! I took a hard look at the content of the video, and the person on camera wasn't me. I sounded like I was reading a teleprompter, and I didn't let my personality shine.

I then began filming thirty-second PR and marketing tips in my car and home with my iPhone, and all the sudden, I was getting thousands of views and engagement on my social media. I started to get clients just because of those videos. Why? They were short, I was more comfortable, and they looked authentic. Authenticity is so important in PR, marketing, and social media.

When you are doing videos or an interview, it's all about telling a story. Jerry Burke, the executive producer at Newsmax, once told me that when you are on camera, pretend that you are telling a conversation at a cocktail party and people are on the outside looking in the window dying to get in and hear your story. He reminded me to smile and pretend I'm talking to a friend, not millions of strangers.

Videos will also help you establish yourself as an expert in your industry, and when journalists research you, they will see you are constantly writing, putting out videos, and engaging with what is going on in your industry. They want the person who is *the* expert. This could be the one thing that helps you land national media exposure.

I was putting out a Tip of the Day Monday through Friday, and people were still watching. In October of 2018, I had posted a video about reputation management in response to a national news story. I happened to pitch one of my clients to a national news network and then followed up with a pitch for myself. I mentioned that I am always available to talk about branding, marketing, public relations, and reputation management if they need an expert to weigh in on the news of the day. Wouldn't you know that within a few minutes, I heard back from the host of the show, and he said he saw my Tip of the Day and they were looking for an expert to weigh in on the subject. Holy cow, I just landed my first national television news hit—all because they saw my video and I pitched them at the right time!

From then on, they asked me to be on a weekly branding segment. It was every Wednesday for five minutes. I was beyond thrilled and scared to death. I also knew how big of an opportunity this was for my brand. I could have easily Skyped in from my home, but I decided to make the three-hour commute to New York City to be in the studio. I was not getting paid. It cost me money to do it. I had to take the train and get a babysitter, all for a five-minute segment. I was taught early on by my parents that you have to work hard for what you want and, sometimes, you work for free. It will pay off—and it did. Six months later, I was asked to be a contributor for the network. From there, I was asked to fill in as a news anchor. My dream at nine years old had finally come to reality. I was a national news anchor, not at 25 but at 43. It happened because of a culmination of many things, but I believe it was because of my continuous video tips, blogs, small press exposure, and willingness to be available and work hard.

Once you have gained your experience through local and industry news and you have put yourself out there through articles and videos, you are now ready to pitch yourself or your company to the national media.

# How to Find National Media Contacts

Finding contacts in the national media takes a little bit of digging. If you have a budget set aside, you can purchase media software such as Cision or Meltwater. They are media databases and have the contact information for many reporters, bookers, producers, and editors. A few other ways you can locate contact information are through Twitter, LinkedIn, and Google. For TV news, you are going to pitch the bookers. For national print, you will look for editors and writers. You can also call the news outlet and ask who the bookers are. Keep in mind that each show has a set of bookers. If you have any contacts in the shows that you are looking to get on, you can also ask them who their bookers are.

## National Media Wants Experts

Similar to local news, national news is all about getting experts to weigh in on topics. Depending on the topic, they too may want to interview you the same day, but if it's not breaking news, they tend to schedule things out for the next day. However, you should always be prepared to talk the same day you send the pitch.

When I sit in on meetings for shows that I anchor, the number-one thing the network bookers are trying to do is set up guests. They want experts to talk about every newsworthy topic. From doctors to economists, whatever's going on in the world, they want an expert to explain it for the viewer.

National news outlets like the Today Show, ABC, NBC, Fox News, and Newsmax have bookers who are in charge of each show. Just like the assignment editors in local news, the bookers are the ones who you want to get to know. They work with the producers to schedule guests on the shows. The same applies to national news as it does with local news. If they ask you to be on a segment, you want to accept and make yourself available.

When I was writing this exact chapter, I received a text from a booker at Newsmax. I was sitting on the beach in Florida with one focus: to write this book. I was away from my family and told my clients that I was off the grid. The booker wanted me to be on his show in two hours. Yup, two hours! I looked at the text for a few minutes without responding. I thought to myself, *I need to focus on this book, I need to write, take a shower, and do my hair and makeup. Plus, I must prepare for the segment.* I honestly didn't want to do it, but I was writing how you shouldn't turn down an opportunity and this was a huge one. I knew the book could wait. I wore the same dress that I wore the other day. I got my butt off the beach and pulled myself together. I'd make it work—and I did because that's what you do if you want media attention.

# PRO TIP

Guerin Hayes, Producer at NBC

*"The national media is always looking for a voice in a story. It's hard for us to find that person who is in a story. We even use social media to look for people who may be impacted by something in the news. If you can think about a story that is generating a buzz and you have a person that brings a perspective to it, you have done the work for the network.*

*Conversationally pitch the story. It doesn't have to be long: "Hey, have you heard that story about such and such? I have a woman who was impacted by that and is available to talk today on camera or later this week. Let me know if you are interested." Many times, by having an available guest, you make the segment happen. As far as talking points, they can feel scripted, but if you have gone over possible questions, you should prepare for the interview in that sense.*

*Some things to keep in mind about how the news works is the producer is responsible for talking to the reporter and knows how to handle a lot of things a reporter does not. The reporter is busy writing or being on air, so your best chance of getting your message to the reporter is through the producer. You can email the producer and send them pictures or videos to see if it helps in producing the story or that you will mention something that could use the picture you are sending. You can also talk to the reporter after the interview and tell them you have a picture of something you mentioned or that you sent the producer some video. If you have some helpful information, try and email it because papers are left in cars or put in bags. A document that can be searched and printed in the office and shared over email is best. When the camera crew shows up at your house, they will set up away from the windows or close the blinds. Light is the enemy for a photographer, and they will take it upon themselves to move chairs and find a spot in a corner or in front of something that reflects your job or who you are. If you want, you can decorate a bookshelf with things you want in the background, have the chairs removed, and tell them you have a spot available if it works.*

*"I have had many guests over the great years, but the ones that stick out are the ones that bring insight and access to a story. I had a group of veterans in a piece that was dealing with the lack of comradery after coming back stateside. We followed an organization that brings the soldiers together for a bonding weekend that included bonfires and yoga as well as river rafting. We got to follow the guys and talk to them about their experiences and what it was like to be around their old units. Sarah Verardo of the Independence Fund allowed us access to the retreat, and we were able to tell the story uniquely from an insider's perspective. While she was in the story, it was the story she pitched and the interviews we had with the veterans that made it such a great piece. If you can get your story out and allow the reporter, producer, and camera person access, you will make a big impact."*

There's one important thing to keep in mind: there is always the chance of breaking news. You may be booked to do a segment. You prepare, you tell everyone on social media, you do your hair and makeup, and you sit in front of the camera ready for them to take you to life—and then the producer tells you that they have to cut you because of breaking news. This happens a lot, but do not get frustrated.

There have been many times that I was ready to go on live TV and I would get bumped for breaking news, a press briefing, or another reason. It's all part of television, and you have to roll with the punches and have fun with it.

I was in a meeting with the team from a national news show, and the booker was amazed at how so many of the guests voiced their anger that they were bumped due to breaking news. Let's just say the booker wasn't happy and those guests weren't back on again. Always be appreciative and let the booker/producer know that you understand how news works. I promise you they will appreciate and remember that.

# PRO TIP:

Guerin Hayes, Producer at NBC

*"Shows love to plan. They have to fill that rundown for the allotted time, but they also have to cover news conferences or breaking news. When an event goes long, guests get 'killed' from the show or 'floated' on standby. The White House briefing can start late, and they may ask the guest to keep talking, but if the White House briefing starts, then the guest is left in limbo or told they are no longer on the show. Especially if news comes out of a briefing, then they need to switch gears and react. This could benefit the guest because they are available and we may need to be contact them last minute. If you are an expert on economics and the White House is pushing an economic stimulus, your phone will start ringing, and you are the most popular person all of a sudden. Having a strong signal also dictates how a show operates. Let's say they are taking a reporter in the field and their signal drops out; then, the show has to pivot. The executive producer needs to go somewhere, and they will ask you to come back or stay on in case their signal drops off. The EP always needs a backup plan, especially with Zoom or Skype interviews being the new norm. Also, shows are divided into hours, so one show producer may float you to the bottom of the rundown, keep you there, and try to make time for you. They will start by cutting things in their rundown to make that time. There may be a forty-second tell that the anchor was set to read, but the line producer can cut it and keep looking for places so there is enough time to get to you at the end of the show. This may mean you get only one minute, so make it count and get your points in quickly because they will cut you off before the next hour so the anchor can sign off and handoff to the next show."*

## Standing Out and Going Viral

The national media likes to tell stories about brands, companies, or people doing something different. How are you standing out? What is creating buzz? Is it going viral?

How do you go from only being known in your local market to being seen all over the world? It starts with the pitch and builds from there.

I had heard about this local camp that helps gold-star families (families who have lost loved ones in combat operations), veterans, and children with disabilities. They all can come together and take advantage of wakeboarding, a ropes course, zero-entry pools, and so much more. It's a place for them to be normal and to not be judged by anyone. I was amazed at what this camp was doing and how they were helping people. I just had to let the media know about this so the world could hear about their story. I drafted a pitch to Fox News because I knew they liked to do military/veteran stories.

Here is the pitch I sent to one of the producers at Fox News:

> Hello Megan,
>
> I hope that you are doing well. A camp for wounded veterans and children with disabilities is slated to open in June in Virginia Beach. JT's Camp Grom, a kind facility on the east coast, is being built in Virginia Beach. The seventy-acre site is an adventure camp with rope courses, lakeside trails, and fitness activities. Wounded veterans, gold-star families, and children with disabilities will soon have a place to come together and experience an adventure like no other. Click here to see.
>
> The camp is being made possible because of a group of young men called "Virginia Gentlemen" who raised the twenty million dollars to build the facility. The founder, a former Naval Officer, had always wanted to create a place for wounded veterans and children. It started with a dream, and he has made it into a reality. The foundation president and

the families who were in the video, including Jason Redman, are available to talk about the camp.

Let me know your thoughts!

*Warm Regards,*

*Alison*

Within a week, I heard from Carley Shimkus, an anchor and reporter for Fox News. The producer had forwarded her the pitch, and she was interested in going to Virginia to do the story. We set up a call with the field producer, and within a month, Carley and her producer were on a plane to Virginia to shoot the story.

Before they arrived at the camp, I ensured we had the key stakeholders, the community being served was represented for the interview, and the news crews had access to what is called "b-roll" (the video needed of people doing things relevant to the story). Communication with the reporter and producer is key in this. It is extremely important to know who they want to interview in advance and ensure that they will have access to conduct those interviews promptly. Carley and her producer were only there for that day, so we needed to make sure that everyone was available and willing to be interviewed. Besides, we made sure that they had a video to cover the voice of the reporter: the more video, the better—in a case like this. For example, if the reporter is talking about the ropes course, you want to make sure that you have people on the ropes course for the crew to film.

When Carley and her producer arrived at the camp, we coordinated the interviews to fit their schedule and allowed them the space to do their job, but we were just an earshot away if they needed anything.

After a few hours, they conducted four interviews and were on their way back to New York, but it wasn't done yet. A few days later, I got a call from the producer. She was putting the story together and realized they needed more b-roll. This is where you can truly help the media and make a lasting impression. I was able to gather a few folks together to go back to the camp to get them playing basketball and fishing. I filmed them with my iPhone and sent them back to the producer within a few hours. She was so appreciative and was able to use the video to edit the story together. The next week, we got word the story was going to air in a few days, and that gave us time to promote it on social media. The camp, those involved, all of the family and friends of the camp, and my agency promoted the story on social media.

The story aired on a Monday at 7:00 a.m., and the response for the camp was *amazing*. They were receiving tons of donations, and many people were asking about how they could help the camp and get involved.

We made sure to personally thank Carley and her producer for the great story they did, and we have since kept in touch with them about any follow-up stories.

This is a prime example of how a small, local non-profit can get national attention. All it takes is a good story, outreach to the right media contact, and coordination.

# Say Thank You

Even if your segment gets cut for breaking news, take the time to send an old-fashioned thank-you note. Emails and text messages are great, but there is something to be said about getting a personalized thank-you card in the mail.

If you have the opportunity to be interviewed by a journalist or were booked for a show, take the time to send them a thank you note. It will go a long way! Getting on national media takes a lot of hard work and time, but it is very possible for every brand and expert.

Start small, create content, be authentic, be persistent, and say yes. Say yes to every opportunity!

# Chapter Roundup

- Write. Write. Write
- Film Informative Videos
- Tell Your Story
- Know How the Media Works
- Stand Out and be Different

# Chapter 10
# How to Write a Killer Press Release

*"Public relations are a key component of any operation in this day of instant communications and rightly inquisitive citizens." – Alvin Adams*

The press release is dying, and I predict they will be extinct within the next ten years, so why am I telling you how to write a killer press release? For now, there is still a time and a place for them.

If you are a public company and have a major announcement, such as a merger, new CEO, new owner, or recall, a press release is recommended

If you're a private company, a press release comes in handy if you've won awards, merged with another company, had an event or grand opening, made some new hires, or were awarded newsworthy promotions. Keep in mind that these press releases usually will be picked up locally or by industry media.

The key to writing a press release is to keep it simple, short, and include the most important information:

1.  When writing a press release, include the five 'Ws': who, what, when, where, and why. At the top of the page, include your contact information, email, and cell number. This is a very important part. You would be surprised how many people forget this!
2.  Your headline should be in a larger font and should sum up what the release is about: for example, "XYZ Company Announces New CEO, John Smith."

3. Put the most important information in the first paragraph and, as I always say, think like a journalist. Why would the reader or viewer care about this story?

4. If you have videos or images, include them in the press release.

5. Keep this to one page. This is very important. Journalists get hundreds of emails a day, and they don't have time to go through a two-page press release.

6. When emailing the press release, copy and paste it in the body of the email. Many media organizations see attachments as spam.

7. This is *the* most important: the subject line in your email needs to draw the attention of the journalist. It has to stand out, but you shouldn't exaggerate or use exclamation points. Keep it simple but attention grabbing.

Here's an example of a press release that generated media requests all over the United States:

Press Release
January 9, 2019
Contact:
Alison Maloni
Alison May Public Relations
***-***-**** or Alison@alisonmaypr.com

## RAPE VICTIM AND FATHER RELAUNCH NEW ANTI-RAPE APP TO SAVE LIVES AND COLLECT EVIDENCE

### *bSafe* App with Groundbreaking Features

**January 8, 2019** - "I called my brother and shouted on the phone: 'You must help me: Charlene has been raped!' Those are the terrifying words of Rich Larsen, a father who just found out his teenage daughter was raped. In 2012, Rich's daughter, Charlene, was raped by two of her friends. The incident changed his family's lives forever."

Today, Rich and Charlene are working together to prevent other women and families from going through the same nightmare with the world-leading safety and security app *bSafe*. In the fight against rape and sexual abuse, *bSafe* developed voice alarm activation, live streaming, and automatic audio and video recording.

According to RAINN, sexual assaults happen every ninety-eight seconds in the United States. One in five women over eighteen years of age has been raped or assaulted by a person attempting to rape her. At college campuses, this ratio worsens to one in four.

This *bSafe* app is providing brand new opportunities because both audio and video recordings provide new insights into what actually happened.

Users can activate the SOS button by voice, even if their mobile phone is placed inside their pocket, purse, or jacket. Their guardians can see and hear everything in real time through live streaming. Both audio and video recordings record up to five minutes. When activating the SOS button, the guardians will receive an audio alarm, and they will be able to see the user's location and see and hear everything that is happening in real time, no matter where they are. Everything is automatically recorded by using *bSafe's* audio and video system.

Both audio and video recordings are instantly sent to the guardians simultaneously; therefore, no information is lost, even if the perpetrator destroys his victim's mobile phone. *bSafe* has additional features like Follow Me, Fake Call, and Timer Alarm.

For media inquiries, please contact Alison Maloni of Alison May Public Relations. Phone number (123) 456-7890 or email Alison@alisonmaypr.com.

The press release can be a useful tool in helping you get your message out, but you should only use it for particular circumstances. The rest of the time, you will want to write a pitch, which we will explore in the next chapter.

# Chapter Roundup

- A press release is used when you have an announcement, a merger, a new product, a new hire—anything big to tell
- Include the five 'Ws': who, what, when, where, and why
- Keep your press release short and simple
- Use links, video, and images if available
- Send the press release in the body of the email, not an attachment
- Don't forget to include your contact information

# Chapter 11
# The Perfect Pitch

*"I receive dozens of pitches every week on new gadgets, websites, and web services. Each reads pretty much the same way. The email starts, "Hi Amber, I hope this finds you well," followed by four or five paragraphs that are copied and pasted from a traditional press release. These all end up in my trash." - Amber MacArthur, Technology Reporter*

Let's get down the most important part of public relations: writing the pitch. A pitch is different from a press release. It's a condensed version of a press release, and it is the ideal way to reach a journalist and get your story told. However, as you have learned, journalists receive hundreds of emails a day. I would say that 90% of pitches I receive end up in my trash. Here are some of the main reasons why the media is not responding to pitches.

1. The story is not for the right audience or media outlet. This means the publicist or company didn't take the time to research the media outlet.
2. Reporters or bookers are Bcc'd (blind carbon copied) in the email. Reporters want personalized pitches.
3. The pitch sounds like a sales pitch rather than a story.
4. The pitch is too long and doesn't have a great story.

# PRO TIP

John Bachman, Anchor and Sr. Vice President, Content Newsmax

*"Simplicity is a beautiful thing. A good pitch doesn't make you think; it makes you react.*

*I'm always looking for PR pitches that are upfront with you about their objective.*

*That saves me and my team time, and time is a precious commodity, perhaps the most precious commodity in our business besides trust. Follow up as many times as it takes to land the interview or have a reporter or assignment manager give you a definitive no.*

*If you want to be a good guest, look good and sound good.*

*Technology, audio and video-quality, Skypes, Facetimes, and Zooms can be key to landing the interview. Control the things you can: your internet connection, your background image, the tech you use to do your live shots, etc.*

*Invest in a good web cam, mic, lighting, and bandwidth.*

*Individuals also need to sound good and look good too. Let's be honest: appearance on TV is important and television is a visual medium, but beauty is in the eye of the beholder, and what's far more important than physical appearance, from the audience's perspective, is that a guest looks comfortable, competent on the topic, and professional, being appropriately dressed for the topic. Plumbers don't wear suits, so don't have a client who's a plumber wear a suit to an interview.*

*Here are some do's and don'ts in the world of TV:*

- *Do have thick skin.*

- *Do be persistent.*

- *Don't hold grudges or keep score.*

- *Don't give up.*

*Reporters and news people are deadline driven and can be rude, curt, and unappreciative, so don't take anything personally.*

*Don't over-promise and under-deliver.*

*It's better to start small, get a few small wins, and build that relationship.*

*Before long, reporters will be calling you for help and advice.*

*I have several stories about a pitch that I received, but a good reporter always protects his sources, so I won't share their secrets here.*

*I kid, I kid. I don't remember the story specifically, but I do remember giving a PR rep a curt blow-off rejection and then regretting it when I saw the story was on another network— and it was really good. I was one of those abrupt dismissive reporters too.*

*To the PR rep's credit, she didn't hold a grudge and accepted my apology without conditions. We've had a great working relationship ever since."*

A pitch is your story. The keyword here is *story*. Public relations is all about storytelling. Journalists are storytellers, and their goal is to relay an impactful story to their audience. A pitch is your story summed up in a couple of sentences with key talking points. Why is your story important to reporters and their readers/viewers? What is the takeaway? What are you doing that's different? Did something just happen in the world that you can talk about? If so, tell the media.

The media loves studies and stats. If you can include a recent study or statistic in your pitch, that will help your story.

**Here's an example of a pitch that we sent to a local news outlet for a client:**

Email Subject Line: 'New Year's Resolution Story: Ditch the Scale'

Hello Brittany,

I hope that you had a great holiday with your beautiful new baby. I wanted to reach out to you about a New Year's resolution story.

Millions of people will make a resolution to lose weight, but one exercise physiologist says, this year, it's all about ditching the scale. Ashley Brodeur of Ashley Brodeur Fitness and owner of Active Lifestyle Fitness says that there is a growing trend of people (especially women) ignoring the scale and opting for strength and flexible dieting. She says this is key to being healthy in 2018.

Ashley is available to come on your show to talk about the following:

- Why we should throw out the scale in 2018
- The importance of flexible dieting and why it works
- How adding muscle helps burn more calories
- Demonstration of exercises that viewers can do at home to add muscle, which will burn more calories!
- As you add muscle and lose fat, your body will be changing, but the scale may not.

Here is a recent video from Ashley that has more on this topic: https://youtu.be/bb5rgkFzmhM.

Ashley is a regular contributor to Western Mass News and has been featured in multiple media outlets.

Please let me know if you would like her to be on your show.

There are a few key points in this pitch: I sent it directly to my contact, which I will explain later in the book, but the introduction was personalized. Even if you don't know the reporter, it's important to research her (Twitter is a great source for that) so you can start with something that shows the journalist you know a little bit about her. If you struggle with coming up with something, simply reference a recent story that she did. The goal is to personalize the introduction, so she knows that it's not a mass pitch to everyone.

I then go directly into a current topic that I know she will be doing stories on. I also send it before New Year's so she can plan this one out.

Next, I go into what value Ashely can provide to her viewers and use bullet points. Journalists love bullet points. Again, keep it simple and get to the point. I made sure to include a video of Ashley and remind Brittany that she has been on the station before, so Brittany knows that Ashley is comfortable with television.

And you end it with a simple goodbye.

**Let's talk about the subject line.** This is *the* most important part of the pitch. This is what is going to get the journalist to click on your email.

The focus of your subject line should be specific as to why reporters should be interested in what you are pitching.

**Ask yourself these questions when writing your subject line:**

- Will they benefit from reading my email?
- What will they learn?
- Is my product or service going to be of interest to their audience?

**Here are some examples of subject lines:**

- Female Tech Exec Runs Fifty-Five Miles Through Lion Territory
- Nike Makes a Huge Mistake for Their Brand, Expert to Weigh In
- Five Recipes to Make on the Grill during the Heatwave
- Pets Dying from Toxic Algae
- Debunking the 'Eight Glasses of Water a Day' Myth
- Home Prices Expected to Rise, Expert to Weigh In
- Danger in the Water: How Swimmers Can Stay Safe
- Lessons About (fill in the blank)

- Heartwarming Story: (Fill in the blank)
- Interview w/Cyber Expert: Rising Risks of Remote Working
- Five Reasons to Use Natural Beauty Products

Back to the pitch, keep in mind that I didn't just send this pitch to one station; I sent personal pitches to all the television stations in Ashley's market along with national outreach. I did individual pitches for each outlet. It is a bit of work, but it does pay off in the end.

If you don't hear back from them, I recommend that you follow up with an email within the next day or two. If they do not get back to you, it's okay. Go back to the drawing board and come up with another pitch that you think will be important to the media outlet's audience.

# PRO TIP

Jen Berson, Jeneration PR

*"I have always operated from the premise that 'the worst they can say is no, but they can't ever say yes unless you try!' Put yourself out there. Share your story! The media is always looking for interesting stories to tell. Why not have it be yours?!"*

# Chapter Roundup

- Keep your pitch short and simple
- Use bullet points, stats, and studies if applicable
- Think like a journalist. Why is this story important?
- Write an eye-catching subject line
- Follow up within days. If you don't hear back, move on

# Chapter 12
# Establishing Relationships with Journalists

*"The key is developing a relationship so it never seems like stalking. I appreciate it when I can say, 'Thanks, but no thanks. Maybe next time.' Pushing for a yes but leaving room for the reporter, producer, or assignment manager room to say no is important.*

*It might mean rejection this time, but when included with a follow up that includes something like, "Can I contact you in the future with other pitches?" I will always say yes to that, and viola — a relationship has started."*

*- John Bachman, Anchor and Sr. Vice President, Content Newsmax*

I remember when I was a local news reporter, frantically working to get my stories written to turn in for editing, living on coffee, and barely having time to eat. We had a deadline and had to get the story on air by news time. Journalists are up against the clock, and with digital media, you don't have all day to get a story together you only have hours.

When I talk about building a relationship with a journalist, it's not based on lunches, coffee, or meetings. It's based on giving them exactly what they need: being available, grateful, and understanding.

## Show them Some Love

The main social media platform that journalists use is Twitter, and the biggest compliment you can give them is to share their stories. This will be extremely important once you get coverage from journalists as they will now be following you.

**Give them What they Need**

Once you hear from a journalist who wants to interview you, it's great if you can provide them with images or videos that relate to the story. If they come to your company to interview, you need to ensure that you have your product or anything that relates to your story available to be filmed.

If you are going to be interviewed, giving journalists talking points about your segment is gold. This gives them a more in-depth idea of what you are going to talk about. Many times, they build the introduction and questions around the talking points.

## PRO TIP

Seth Denson, Co-Founder & Chief Strategist at GDP Advisors

*"Being available when the media needs you is extremely important—it really does two things: first, it gives the producers the confidence that they can call on you and you'll be there for them when the news breaks, and second, it gives you as many at-bats as possible. Out of sight, out of mind is never more applicable than it is in the national media spotlight. Until such a time as you know you're getting prime time hits regularly, you take the hits you're offered, and you take them with a smile— they will lead to a better you and better opportunities."*

## Be Available

I touched on this earlier in the book, but I can't stress how important this is: it's all about being flexible with the news. If the media wants to talk to you, I highly suggest that you rearrange your schedule to accommodate them. They may schedule your interview for 9:00 a.m. and have to change it a few times that day. They may book you for tomorrow and then bump you to the next day, and if they have to move your time or cancel, it's important to emphasize how much you understand.

# Thank you

If you only knew the angry emails, social media messages, and voicemails journalists get from readers and viewers—it's a tough job, and it's getting even tougher. That's why it is always nice to receive a thank-you email or note. It makes a huge difference in their day, and when you publicly thank them on social media by sharing their article or story, it's a huge win for you. Journalists love people sharing their stories, and it goes a long way.

# Stay in Touch

In the world of news, yesterday feels like a week ago. Once journalists finish one story, they are focused on the next. It's always a good idea to touch base with them by emailing a friendly hello and reminding them you are always available to talk about specific topics (make sure to list them out). Once they do a story with you, the chance of doing another one increases. Stay in front of them and share their stories on social media.

Public Relations is all about relationships, and it does take a bit of time, but you can start by following the reporters, editors, and bookers on Twitter. This is where journalists live and spend a lot of their time. The key to journalists' hearts is when you share their stories. It's a huge compliment, so if there is a story that is of interest to you, re-tweet it with a quick write up.

# PRO TIP

Gary Brown, VP Meredith Broadcasting. Gary is a former station manager and news director in several markets across the country.

*"The most effective public relations folks have relationships with news managers and content decision-makers, but you have to realize you both have jobs and no matter how good the relationship is, you may not win every time.*

*When I was a news director in smaller markets, the PR folks for a major hospital chain made sure to meet me. At the time, they always stopped by my office in the newsroom when they would come to the station to meet with sales. They made sure that I was invited to every sponsored event. They made sure that when I was thinking of a story, they were my first call instead of their competitor. It's all about being top of mind. It's not always about pitching but just building the relationship. In PR and news, it's all about relationships. Always have a plan. Know this will not happen overnight and will require work and time, but it will all be worth it if you are their first call or email."*

# Chapter Roundup

- Don't be afraid to reach out to journalists and follow up
- Respond quickly to reporters' requests and give them what they need
- Understand their deadlines and be flexible with your schedule
- Give them more stories you think they would like to cover
- Say thank you with a note card and show them love on Twitter

# Chapter 13
# Preparing for Your Interview

*"Failing to prepare is preparing to fail."* - *John Wooden*

You've made it. You pitched your story. The media responded. You are booked for an interview. Now, it's time to prepare.

## Digital Media

Digital media interviews could be by phone, Zoom, or email. Either way, you should write out your talking points that you want to get across and research everything that you need to know, especially if it's about a newsworthy topic. You should also send your talking points to the editor or reporter. This not only helps them prepare for the interview, but it helps you get ready too. You will want to make sure you know everything and anything about your brand in case they ask. Don't ramble in your answers. Keep them simple and to the point.

## Television

TV interviews need a bit more prep work as it can be more nerve-wracking, but the more you do, the more comfortable you will get with them.

You will do the same preparation as you would do for a phone interview, but you want to focus on what, in television, we call "speaking in soundbites." The purpose of soundbites is to help people remember what you said and why you said it. When being interviewed, include the original question in your answer. Repeating the reporter's question in your answer creates a soundbite that stands on its own.

If you have stats or studies and you would like them to make a graphic, you can ask if that is possible. TV news loves graphics and video options.

Make it interesting. You want to stand out, so people notice and remember what you say. Personal stories are always great as long as you can keep them short. Producers also love when your personality shines and you bring the energy.

# PRO TIP

Guerin Hays, Producer at NBC

*"Know that you are the guest, be prepared to answer questions, and do not correct the anchor in a way that makes them look bad. There is an art to correcting someone who is not as familiar with a topic as you are: 'You're right about that, but we are finding that this is happening now, and many people are surprised.' This corrective response makes the anchor feel like he is not alone in his opinion and that he is informing others. Be prepared to be flexible. You may be dropped from a show, but another booker sees you in the system and may want to add you to another show. A producer working on a piece may even ask you to stay after the show so he can interview you on a topic. Nothing is better than having a guest in the office or available instead of having to find another one and set it up."*

Know your message. What's the one main point you want to get across? Keep it simple and concise, and above all, speak with confidence.

# Practice.

Stand in the mirror or record yourself. It sounds silly, but it's the best way to prepare. Keep rehearsing until you feel comfortable with your statements. Go over what you want to say with colleagues since they can give you honest feedback.

# Storytelling.

Think of your interview as if you are having a conversation with a friend. You are simply telling them a story that you are passionate about.

If you have a taped interview, you can always ask to re-do the answer. Generally, the reporter will allow you to do that. Also, at the end of the interview, many reporters will ask if there is anything else that you would like to add; this is your chance to get in something that you may have missed. If they don't ask you, feel free to let them know that you missed one point, and always look at the reporter, not the camera.

A live interview can sound scary, but the goal is to get the fear out of your mind. As long as you are prepared, you will rock it. Before your interview, ask your contact how long the segment is. This way you will know how much to prepare for.

Unfortunately, you can't ask for the questions beforehand, so you really don't know what the reporter is going to ask you. Live TV is like a live wire: you never know what can happen, and that is why it's really important to get your feet wet on local TV before you make your way to the network. It's also important to be prepared.

# PRO TIP

Seth Denson, Co-Founder & Chief Strategist at GDP Advisors

*"First, recognize that during a live hit/interview, anything can happen. The more you think about the 'what ifs' before going live, the better off you'll be.*

*I remember the first time this happened was when I was prepared to go live for an interview on Fox News. I knew the idea of what we were going to cover on the segment, but as is almost always the case, I wasn't exactly sure which direction the host was going to take the conversation. About forty-five seconds until we were to "go live," the producer spoke into my ear that they're going to change the segment and instead of it being me with the host one-on-one, they were going to bring in another subject-matter expert that was going to debate me as they were taking a different position on the matter. In the end, the segment went well, but nonetheless, I learned a valuable lesson that I always must prepare to respond to the counterpoint, even if there's a high likelihood that I'll not be debating (unless given the heads up, of course).*

*Another story was one where I knew I was going to be debating, and instead of debating the other guest, instead, I listened as the host started to debate the other guest. The issue was the host was wrong—her facts were wrong. When the host turned to me to support her claims, I knew I couldn't do it. I also didn't want to embarrass the host on live television, on their show, in front of millions of viewers... so I pivoted. I took the conversation a different direction, saving me, the host, and ultimately the network a lot of embarrassment. In short, always have a pivot."*

*The last situation I'll share was when I once was doing an interview with a host and instead of discussing the topic I was under the impression we would discuss, she instead decided to ask me questions about a topic I knew very little about and certainly could not consider myself an expert on. Needless to say, I handled the conversation well, shared what my opinion on the matter was, and gracefully got through the segment. Here's the lesson learned: first, always know the "news of the day," even if it's not your subject-matter expertise. Hosts are regularly pulling current events into the conversation, so you'd better be prepared to provide an opinion. Second, in the absence of known facts and expertise, provide a humble opinion and state that. Do not fake it—you'll be called out. Opinions are subjective, but facts are undeniable. When in doubt, don't put yourself in a position to go against the undeniable, and it's always okay to say, "I'm not really an expert in that area, but here's what my current opinion is..."*

*There is no substitution for being prepared. Certainly, you don't want to overprepare to the extent you are scripted and robotic, but you should also know your stuff. Second, be authentic—the world is filled with enough false information calling itself reality. You will endear yourself to the audience if you are just yourself in your simplest form, and finally, always tell the truth—if you do, you won't have to remember what you say... because <u>the truth never changes</u>!"*

# Camera-Ready

Once you have prepared what you want to say, it's time to get ready for the camera. This goes for men and women. The lights are harsh, and you will want to add a bit of color and get rid of shine. Guys, you should get a foundation, under-eye concealer, and powder. Yes, seriously! MAC makeup has great camera-ready makeup. I suggest that you go to the MAC counter, tell them that you will be on TV, and see what they suggest. If you go to national TV, check with the producer to see if they will have hair and makeup. I always recommend that you go to the studio camera ready.

Ladies, I also suggest that you get a makeup consult with someone who is experienced in television makeup. You will always want to put more makeup on than you think you need. As for your hair, if you are booked for a television segment and have time, it's always a good idea to go to a hair salon and get a blowout. That way, you don't have to worry about doing your hair, and it will look professionally done.

When COVID-19 hit, I had to begin doing the news from my living room, and I couldn't rely on my fairy godmother, Maureen Walsh, to fix me up. She told me exactly what shades of foundation and concealer I needed, along with tips on how to make my eyes look bigger. She told me everything to buy, from eyelashes to lipstick; she was my hero. I will say that no matter what I do, it never looks as good as when Maureen does it!

# PRO TIP

Maureen Walsh, makeup artist

*"The most important thing about getting ready for television news is to have specific makeup for the studio lights.*

*This can be executed by makeup techniques which can make the skin look flawless and smooth, matte by applying foundation. The use of concealer to cover darkness in the under-eye area, to cover redness, rosacea, acne, scars, etc. Applying powder to set all of the makeup application to give a matte finish. The goal also is to look polished and pulled together—not to appear pale, washed out, or too shiny. This is achieved with a balanced application of eye shadow, eye liner, mascara, false lashes, bronzer, blush, lip liner lipstick, and lip gloss. For the face to not appear flat /one dimensional, applying a contouring and highlighting technique helps pronounce facial features and overall bone structure by emphasizing cheekbones, eye sockets, and jawlines. This can be achieved by specifically applying a darker matte bronzer under the bones to sculpt the face"*

# Advice for Women

Maureen says that women should approach their makeup for TV by keeping their regime the same. "Just add more concealer, more foundation, and more powder to set the makeup and to keep the skin looking matte. If no powder is applied, the skin will look shiny, giving an oily or perspired appearance. Many times, people are feeling a little rush of adrenaline or anxiety before going on TV—you never want to appear sweaty. You always want to look confident, like things are going your way."

# Advice for Men

"The skin on a man's face—especially the beard area—the camera will pick this up as appearing shadowed or darker. The goal is to balance the skin tone by covering up the beard area, concealing redness, brightening the under-eye area, and then powdering the face to take down the shine. One final touch I recommend is applying a matte bronzer contouring under the jawbone and along the hairline and cheekbones," Maureen Walsh

## Product Recommendations

Maureen recommends investing in good professional products that are highly pigmented.

Joe Blasco
RCMA
Makeup Forever
MAC
INGLOT

She says you should also invest in good brushes and keep them clean after every use. "Always approach makeup applications with clean brushes. This trick will result in the makeup application looking beautifully blended, effective, and sharp. I highly recommend anyone who is unsure about makeup products or techniques to please consult a professional and book yourself a makeup lesson! Makeup artists love to share their skills and recommend the best products and colors for flawless skin," says Maureen.

# Wardrobe

Your wardrobe is just as important. I always tell men to wear a fitted sports jacket and a crisp shirt. Stick to basic solid colors and wear what looks good on you and fits appropriately.

For women, stick to solid colors that pop and work with your skin tone. Stay away from patterns and flowy tops and dresses. Wear what you feel good in and makes you stand out. If you start to get regular appearances on the news, Rent the Runway has a monthly subscription service in which you can get several dresses, and once you return the dresses, you can order more. This is a huge money saver! The best part is you can cancel any time and you don't have to spend a fortune on dresses you will only wear a few times.

The goal is to look yourself with a little bit more glam, so you glow on television. The more interviews you do, the better you will get, and it will eventually seem like a piece of cake.

# PRO TIP:

Guerin Hayes, Producer NBC

*"Do not wear an outfit that is distracting. I've seen guys with black shirts and crazy ties or women with striped patterns that don't show up on TV. Make sure your outfit is TV friendly. Green can disappear with background. White and black patterns can be too busy for a TV signal and show up as odd lines on TV.*

*"The more you do your interviews, the more comfortable you will be with live TV segments, but no matter how confident you are, preparation is key. It's also important to be knowledgeable in what is going on in your industry or the news cycle since a journalist could throw a curveball question."*

# Chapter Roundup

- Prepare for your interview by practicing in the mirror
- Know your message and the key points you want to convey
- Wear camera-friendly makeup, such as Mac Studio
- Men, makeup for you too. Under-eye concealer and powder is a must
- Wear solid bright colors that work with your skin tone

# Chapter 14: Maximizing Your Press Coverage

*"Nobody counts the number of ads you run; they just remember the impression you make."*
 – Bill Bernbach, advertising pioneer and founder of DDBl.

You have made it! All of your hard work to get press coverage has paid off, and unlike advertising where you can't share it on social media, you can promote the heck out of your media coverage.

Before your story is even live, you can pre-promote the coverage. If you are filming with a television station, have a colleague take a photo of you getting interviewed. Then, share on social media that you will be on that media outlet with that specific reporter. Tag the media outlet and the reporter in all of your posts. Be sure to use Instagram and Facebook stories for this as well—and, of course, post on Twitter also. Remember, nearly every journalist is on Twitter. If you tag the reporter and news outlet, they could potentially retweet it. Now, you are in front of all of their followers.

If you have a live segment coming up, do the same and tell everyone to tune in.

Once your story airs, ask for the link to the segment so you can share it on social media. Many times, the media outlet will have already put it on social media. This goes for digital media and podcasts. Encourage your colleagues, friends, and family to share the story on their platforms too.

You can put your media segments on your website and share them in an email blast to your list of contacts. This is where your public relations can help you build your credibility. Every time you share you are in a magazine or on the news, your followers will see, people on your email list will read the story, and you will start to gain followers on social media. It is a slow process, but it does build your reputation. Will public relations have people knocking down your doors immediately to buy your product or do business with you? No, not right away, but it is building awareness, credibility, authenticity, and a desire from your audience to see and hear more. This is where you start to see your public relations efforts pay off. Perception becomes reality.

I truly know that if you follow these steps, your brand will be taken to the next level, and while this is not easy and you must put in the work, the reward is so worth it. You have an important story to tell, and your audience will benefit from what you have to say or what your company does. Trust the process and believe this will take you to where you want to be. I will see you on the news!

# Chapter Roundup

- Promote your interview before it airs on social media
- Tag the journalist and media outlet on all platforms, especially Twitter
- Ask the media outlet for a clip of your segment so you can promote it
- Post your story on your website and include the link in your email blasts

# Chapter 15:
# Everybody Needs a Crisis Plan

*"Don't wait until you have a crisis to come up with a crisis plan."*
*- Phil McGraw*

Every company will at some point be faced with a crisis situation. 2020 taught us a lot about dealing with the unexpected. We never could have imagined we would be going through a pandemic and a national shutdown. Whether it is directly or indirectly, a business reaction and response will impact the brand.

Imagine this: you spend years working to maintain a stellar reputation. You work countless hours building your brand and business, but within ten minutes, your company's name is all over the media and internet. Your five-star reviews have gone to one-star, and the media is knocking on your door. You are now dealing with a major public relations crisis, and it's all because of one thing that you or your employee may have written or said.

That scenario happens all of the time to large corporations and small businesses. Take Google, for example. Remember when a senior software engineer wrote a ten-page "manifesto" condemning Google's diversity efforts and claiming men are biologically more predisposed to working in the tech industry than women? That memo was leaked, and within hours, it was all over the media. Google's CEO was then scrambling to address the issue internally and externally.

You don't have to be a major corporation to have a PR nightmare on your hands. We have seen countless public figures and thought leaders receive negative press for something they said, did, or posted on social media. Everything you do or say can be shared on social media. If you think an email is safe, think again.

# PRO TIP

Mark Vargas, Political Strategist

*"I've been in the middle of Category Five media frenzy—and it happened on February 18, 2020, the day I went to Denver, CO, to pick up former Illinois Governor Rod Blagojevich from prison only hours after President Donald J. Trump had commuted his sentence. When I landed in Denver and turned on my phone, I had nearly 500 phone text messages and emails from members of the press. There were news helicopters in the air and hovering above the prison, and a dozen reporters were lined up across the street waiting to catch a glimpse of the former governor walking out of prison for the first time as a free man. I've also found myself in situations with a high-profile client when a simple sit-down interview is suddenly breaking news on nearly every mainstream media outlet—and it's up to you to fix it and change the narrative quickly!*

*The first rule of thumb, if you find yourself in these types of situations, is don't panic! Generally speaking, these stories will only last a news cycle or two, and then, the press moves on. That's when you can feel your blood pressure go back to semi-normal levels again. Like a tornado, it's chaotic for a day or so, but then, before you know it, the media is distracted by another story. The news cycle is always moving on to another shiny object.*

*The second rule of thumb is to shift the narrative. In that brief window, it seems like the whole world is listening to you—take advantage of that, get your message out, and leverage media interviews, opinion pieces, social media, and blogs to get your message out to the masses quickly. If you can, get surrogates and supporters out there speaking up for you as well. Build a coalition of support."*

Everything is under a microscope, and it's up to you as a business owner to think through every decision you make. We are in a digital age where bad news and social shaming spreads like wildfire. It's also up to you to educate your staff about the impact of social media on the business.

Companies need to think about security breaches, bad advertising, miscommunication, a national tragedy, a global pandemic, workplace crime, harassment, discrimination, or CEO or upper management scandals.

Big or small, for profit or not-for-profit, all organizations should have a well-rounded plan in place. A good crisis plan will serve as a guidebook to navigating all situations that could affect the profitability, integrity, or reputation of your organization. The key is to be proactive. A good plan is going to involve putting together a crisis team that will set protocols into motion in the event of a crisis. The team will oversee approvals on public statements, social media management, advertising, and the press.

Putting together a crisis plan is not very difficult; it just takes a bit of time and preparation.

## Be Prepared

Get ahead of the story. The time spent planning for what might happen will help you when a crisis occurs. Think about your industry and what types of events and challenges occur. For example, if you are a restaurant, you will want to plan for potential food poisoning.

- Create a Crisis Communications Team
- Think about what types of things could go wrong
- Assign a spokesperson who will talk to the media
- Include your social media team in the plan
- Talk and train your staff about how they handle the media. All media inquiries should be directed to one person

# Act Fast

Get ahead of the situation as quickly as possible to help diffuse negative responses. Craft your message and speak to the media. If you say no comment, it will look like you are hiding something. If you need to apologize, then it's best to say sorry and own it. The longer you draw things out, the longer it will stay in the media and on social media.

# Monitor Social Media and Other Emails

Assign a team to monitor your social media and mainstream media so you can be aware of what people are saying. Keep track of social media and other media outlet responses in order to stay on top of all the comments and messages. You can communicate most effectively when you know what is being said and by whom.

# Be Transparent

People can see through lies and when you are inauthentic. It is important to be honest in your response. The best way to rebuild and maintain trust is to be honest about what happened. It is also important to communicate the steps you or your company will take to move forward.

Whether you are the CEO of a company or someone who is building their personal brand, it is really important to think about everything you say or do.

Crisis planning is not something many business owners think about or care to spend their time focusing on. However, it can make or break your business. Just remember that social media is not going away. News travels fast. Bad news travels even faster.

# Chapter Roundup:

- A crisis can happen to any company of any size
- Have your plan before you need it
- Get ahead of the crisis
- Don't avoid the media
- Address the situation head on

# Conclusion

Once you start getting quoted in the media and doing television interviews, it is such a great feeling. It's because you are telling your story and sharing your knowledge to people across the world. We don't give ourselves enough credit for how smart we are and what we have to offer to others. We all have a gift, and if we don't share our advice and story, we are doing a disservice to people who need it. When I first started writing and doing videos, I thought no one would care about what I was saying, but I proved myself wrong (which happens a lot). People did care, and they actually were taking my advice and getting press coverage, and then, there were the personal stories that I shared about my eating disorder and being a single mom. So many people reached out to me about how they too were going through that and how I helped them because they knew they weren't alone.

You read this book for a reason. Maybe it was because you want to be on The Today Show or because you changed your career after COVID and were starting over. Whatever the reason, this is your time to build a brand and business you have wanted. This is your time to tell your story and share your advice. You may be scared, scared to put yourself out there in the public eye, scared that you may make a mistake on TV, scared that people will judge you, scared that you don't know enough about your industry—but the benefits far outweigh the risks. Don't let fear get in the way of that. Putting yourself out there in the media and on camera can be scary, but I promise it gets easier. You now have all the tools to do it yourself, and it doesn't need to take up too much of your time. Just like everything else you do in your business, PR should be a part of it. If you make it a priority and take an hour or two each week to focus on pitching, using HARO, and putting yourself and your company out there, you will see results, and in turn, you will attract more people to your business. Everyone deserves to hear from you. It's up to you to tell your story.

# Acknowledgments

I want to start by thanking my three beautiful and extremely patient daughters. McKenna, Addison, and Hannah, everything I do is because of you. When I feel like giving up, I think about who is watching me and how strong the three of you are. You have stood by my side during the toughest times in my life. The early mornings, the late nights, going to New York and leaving you with babysitters more than I wanted to, you supported me through it all. When I decided to add this book to my list of jobs, you didn't complain once. You allowed me the time to work and focus on getting this done. I love you so much for that. I couldn't have done this without your love and support.

To my role model and my mentor since I was nine years old, Brenda Garton Sjoberg, I would not be here if it wasn't for you. You took me under your wing at the small television station in Springfield, Massachusetts, and always encouraged me that I would be a news anchor. Years later, when I got out of the business, you were the one who kept telling me that I should be back on air. Again, because of your advice, I took a chance and made my ultimate dream of being a network anchor come true. Thank you from the bottom of my heart.

This book wouldn't have been possible without some of my amazing clients, friends, and the best people I know in the news business and public relations industry. Seth Denson, Mark Vargas, John Bachman, Jen Berson, Gina DiStefano, Ashley Brodeur, Gary Brown, Sabriana Reilly, Guerin Hayes, Maureen Walsh, Kelsey Olgetree, Susie Ippolito, Mike Tourville, and Bre Kingsbury, you all contributed so much knowledge to this book, and it's because of you that the readers now understand the news business better.

My publisher, Daniel J. Mawhinney & Darlene Shortridge of 40 Day Publishing, thank you for taking a chance on me and guiding me through this process. I don't know how I would have made this book a reality without you. You are truly a blessing.

I also would like to thank Newsmax and my friends at the network. John Bachman took a chance on me and let me come on his show. John, that truly changed my life. Chris Ruddy, thank you for believing in me and allowing me to fill in as an anchor on your shows. Chris, I am forever grateful. Bob Sellers, you sat next to me on the anchor desk and helped me through my first few months, which were terrifying. Thank you for that. Jerry Burke, hold on to your wig. Thank you for having me be a part of your team and sharing your amazing stories.

Maureen Walsh and Jacqui Phillips, thank you for making me look beautiful and for being my therapists in the makeup chair. You add such value to this book. Jacqui, thank you for passing on your knowledge as an author and helping me through this extremely difficult process. Barry Morgenstein, thank you for taking my book cover photo. Your talent is tremendous, and I am honored that you are a part of this. Jade Voight, you made me beautiful for the cover and I can't thank you enough.

I want to thank all of my friends and family who encouraged me to write this book and gave me the confidence to keep going. Your advice resonated with me and allowed me to power through.

Jon Daskam, thank you for believing in me and building up my confidence when I was questioning my ability.

And to my parents, Danny and Sherry Maloni, thank you for your words of support and for encouraging me to follow my dreams.

And finally, I want to thank my mom, Bonnie May Haight. She's been in heaven for forty years now, but she is with me every day. She is my guardian angel and is the reason I have never given up. She is my daily strength and is the voice inside my head that tells me that I can do it and to reach for the stars. Well, I did, Mom, and thank you for watching over me. I love you.

# About Alison Maloni

Alison Maloni is the owner of Alison May Public Relations. A journalist of more than twenty years, Alison is a contributor and anchor for Newsmax. She is also an acclaimed keynote speaker. In front of the camera, a born storyteller, Alison has interviewed hundreds of people, from politicians to well-known experts. Behind the camera, she has garnered media for her clients in outlets such as Entrepreneur Magazine, Forbes, Inc, The Today Show, Newsmax, and Fox News.

Alison is a well-respected publicist among reporters, producers, and editors around the world because of her understanding of what journalists want and need. She has been featured in outlets such as Time Magazine, Daily Worth, Dr. Oz, and Reputation Management.

Alison's real job however is being a mom to three beautiful and intelligent girls. When she is not working or writing, her time is spent with her daughters and traveling as much as she can.

CPSIA information can be obtained
at www.ICGtesting.com
Printed in the USA
BVHW042318031021
618069BV00013B/564